Reclaiming Power in Congregational
and Community Ministry

Reclaiming Power in Congregational and Community Ministry

Creating Shared Power for Effective Ministry

Fritz Ritsch

Foreword by John Wimberly

WIPF *&* STOCK · Eugene, Oregon

To St. Stephen Presbyterian Church in Fort Worth,
Whose power is its wonderful people.

To my amazing family, Margaret, Bennie, and
Sara Caitlin, the source of my joy.

Contents

Contents

Foreword

Consulting with congregations and judicatories over the past thirteen years after decades of pastoring, it has become crystal clear to me that we are in the early stages of a second Reformation. The first Reformation was fueled by Guttenberg's printing press that allowed information to flow freely across Europe. The second Reformation is being fueled by the internet and other technologies that have information streaming freely across the entire world.

Once Luther nailed his Ninety-Five Theses on a church door, there was no going back. Pandora's box was opened. In like manner, once the millennial and Gen-Z generations appeared, questioning every institution prior generations had accepted as givens; growing up in preschools and schools more diverse than the universities boomers attended; and filling the streets to protest George Floyd's death, environmental policies, and more, it was just a matter of time before the contemporary church would have its day of reckoning. That day has come.

Churches of all types today are filled with boomers and a sprinkling of Gen-Xers. As such, their days are numbered. Currently, over 2.6 million boomers die annually in the United States. Unless congregations can find ways to engage the millennial and Gen-Z generations, a small fraction of today's congregations will survive.

However, and it is a huge "however," the task will require the church to reshape its image and practices. The youngest two generations typically describe themselves as "spiritual but not religious." Sounds like Jesus to me. Obviously a spiritual giant, Jesus was also in regular conflict with the religious establishment of his day. I have no doubt that he would be in conflict with the religious establishments of our day.

Since "spiritual but not religious" rings true with Jesus and many of great prophets of the church over the centuries, I'll take two generations that describe themselves in such terms any day, anywhere. If we can't connect their sometimes-nebulous concept of spiritual with the clear vision of God revealed by Jesus, well, we shouldn't be in the business of communicating the Gospel. The search for spiritual depth in the younger generations is as rich a potential field of disciples for today's church as was the large number of people in Europe in the sixteenth century who yearned for more than what the medieval church offered them. Today, the field is once again there for the harvesting.

Fritz Ritsch's book gives congregations an important tool as they devise strategies to engage the younger generations. He talks about the connection between the gospel and power. We need to listen to him. If we won't, I guarantee younger generations will. His models for pursuing social, economic, racial and environmental justice are in sync with what the younger generations are doing.

Most in the younger generations associate the use of power by religious groups with either the religious right or religious left. In other words, they see the church's use of power as partisan politics with a thin theological veneer. Pew and other polling groups have identified this generational antipathy to the use of partisan politics in the church. Younger folks don't want what either the right or left are selling. However, they absolutely want to realize major changes in the way our society is governed and the policies that govern us.

I would add that by becoming partisan in the use of power, we give away what the business community calls our "competitive advantage." Our "competitive advantage" is spirituality and a spiritual understanding of events in the world. We critique all political systems, not just those we oppose. When we focus on a spiritual understanding of power, personal and political, we attract and engage people. When we think we can preach the Democratic or Republican platform better than either party does, we alienate the younger generations.

In my consulting, I constantly hear boomers describe the younger generations as "apathetic." Nonsense. Again, think of the way they flooded the streets during the Black Lives Matter demonstrations or any environmental protest. As important, look at the life choices they are making. It feels like every time I ask a young person what they are planning to study in college, they say something related to the environment. These are young people that care about the future, their future.

To convince these determined young people that the church is on their side, we need a much more nuanced understanding of power than we have been using during my fifty years as a pastor and consultant. Ritsch's book is an important step in that direction. He dissects the church's fear of power and shows how it leads to exercising power in counterproductive ways. He gives specific examples of how power is used and misused in the local church.

Following Ritsch's line of thinking, if we can figure out how to use power without becoming like the power-full, I think the younger generations will take notice. If we can unlock the gospel from the grips of political partisans with the church, I think they will join us. If we can connect the appropriate use of power with personal spiritual development, I think those of us who are boomers can let go of the power we so tightly grip and enjoy the last years of lives watching younger folks use it to continue building God's realm on earth.

John Wimberly
Congregational Consultant
August 2023

1

Welcome to the New World

DOES RELIGIOUS FAITH, A once powerful force shaping the nation, continue to have any power in the mid-twenty-first century?

Many assume that faith's power in the United States is a given, long established, and especially evident today in a particular "Christian" perspective that has come to have vast political power. But many faith traditions that do not embrace the notion of Christian political dominance struggle with feelings of powerlessness.

The Faith Communities Today (FCT) report is a twenty-year study of congregations throughout the United States. It tells us that congregations of all faiths are in trouble. Over twenty years, attendance has halved.[1] Two-thirds of existing congregations are experiencing "changing size disparities with significant financial and resource implications . . . the aging of members and clergy . . . and the decreased involvement of younger generations."[2] The FCT's information was by its own admission dated almost as soon as it was released. It touched on only one year of the three-year COVID-19 outbreak, which has fast-tracked this long-established congregational deterioration.

So, on the one hand, a sectarian brand of Christian faith has made deep and abiding inroads into the seats of American power; and on the other hand, American congregations face a seemingly inevitable tidal wave

1. Thumma, "Twenty Years of Congregational Change," 11.
2. Thumma, "Twenty Years of Congregational Change," 29.

of decline. Many faith institutions consider the partisan religious takeover of political discourse a bad thing, and of course they are unhappy about their own institutional deterioration, but they feel powerless effectively to address either. Many religious groups believe that their job is to work not as dominant, but *equal* partners with other faiths and interest groups to build up our communities and nation, but they find themselves stymied at every turn. Recovering our power to bear witness to a faith that heals, reconciles, and builds bridges in our congregations and communities, is the focus of this book.

Where We Are

Nicholas Kristof writes that "some forty million American adults once went to the church but have stopped going, mostly in the last quarter century."[3] For years there has been debate over what is causing congregational decline and what to do about it. In *Unchristian*, published in 2007, Kinnaman and Lyons of the Barna Group, an evangelical polling group, identified that many millennials had soured on Christianity, considering Christians hypocritical, too engaged in politics, closed-minded toward other faiths, anti-science, over-simplistic, and judgmental and condemning, especially toward LGBTQ people and issues. Ironically, Kinnaman and Lyons found that younger people believed Christians are "unchristian" in the sense that though they say they follow Jesus, they do not abide by the values Jesus stands for.[4] This sixteen-year-old analysis remains relevant: Russell Moore, editor of *Christianity Today,* told the New York Times in December of 2022 that "I find more and more young evangelicals who think the church itself is immoral" leaving the church.[5]

The ironies keep piling up. Polling indicates that 27 percent of Americans who self-identify as Evangelicals *rarely if ever attend church.*[6] Most of these unchurched Evangelicals seem to be practicing their faith by their politics. A recent Pew Survey found that "six percent of White adults . . . began calling themselves born-again/evangelical Protestants between 2016 and 2020," and that "White Americans with warm views toward [Donald] Trump were far more likely than those with less favorable views of the

3. Kristof, "America," para. 5.

4. Kinnaman, *Unchristian*, 29.

5. Goldberg, "Empty," para. 10.

6. Burge, "Evangelical Is Becoming," para. 6.

former president to *begin identifying* [emphasis theirs] as born-again/evangelical Protestants."[7] For them, Evangelical Christianity means the ancient Roman virtue of *pietus*: God, country, family. Today it manifests as Christian nationalism. They pray in the ballot box.

And they've had great success. Even as institutional faith has been steadily declining, ultra-right-wing religiously affiliated institutions have, over the course of the forty years since they embraced an openly political agenda, helped elect several presidents and members of congress, overseen the creation of a six-three majority in the Supreme Court, and overturned *Roe v. Wade*. They have retooled legislative agendas, from town councils up to Congress, to focus on personal moral issues and to undermine a half-century of racial reconciliation. They have driven an overtly conservative Christian agenda to national success even as Christianity itself has experienced a dramatic national decline. The logical outcome is that Christian nationalism will soon be the dominant way to be religious in America.

Rethinking Power

To understand both institutional faith's decline and right-wing political Christianity's great success one must understand *power*. It is my thesis that faith institutions' general failure to understand power and partisan Christianity's overreaching lust for power are at the core of this troubling turn of events; and that if faith institutions reframe power and its purpose, they will experience rebirth, do more good for their communities and world, represent their faith better to a disaffected and disgruntled populace, and offset the extraordinary damage that power-hungry Christian nationalism is doing to our nation's better angels.

Throughout this book, I use the word "power" unapologetically. For many, that is jarring. One reason is our overall discomfort with the word *power*, which we associate with domination and abuse. But power simply means *the ability to act*. I hope to connect power with positive associations so that religious people recognize that *they have the God-given ability to act*, individually and corporately, in their lives and their ministry, to create communities of *shalom*—health, wholeness, togetherness, mutuality, and peace.

"Gifts" and "talents" are words we use in church but are often associated with passivity. Gifts are received and talents are innate. In normal parlance, these words can be disassociated with intentionality, responsibility,

---

7. Smith, "More White Americans," paras. 7, 9.

and accountability. That we experience them as nonthreatening reveals their purpose: they are meant to tame us. As one community organizer/pastor puts it, "A gift or talent not matched with power is essentially useless because it is dormant. It is only valuable when the talent/gift is used in some form of action."[8]

Power, by contrast, is wild, untamed except by the will of the person who wields it. It has far-reaching consequences. It can even get out of control. That's why things that have power are often more amorphous than skills or talents. They can be emotions, attitudes, unconscious systemic norms, character traits—even faith itself. Power, of course, properly directed, is in Christian theology a gift of the Holy Spirit, who is described as untamed: Jesus says, "The wind blows where it chooses; you hear the sound of it, but you do not know where it comes from or where it goes. So it is with the Holy Spirit" (John 3:8).

This book is a guide to faith leaders, clergy and lay, to identify and deal with power dynamics in their congregations and communities and tap into and engage their own power and the power of their congregants, turning them into leaders with a deep investment in their faith, congregation, and community.

This book's guiding principle is community organizing's pursuit of democratic power for the good of diverse communities. In organizing, they speak of two types of power: shared and dominating. *Dominating power* has framed political Christianity's rise to power. *Shared power*, in contrast, doesn't seek to dominate but to unite. This book is a tool for religious leaders and congregations, regardless of their faith tradition, who view unity, diversity, bridge-building, compassion, and love of neighbor as the values God calls them to practice. I call such institutions *unifying congregations*.

Whether you view yourself or your congregation as liberal or conservative or neither; if you believe that faith is best conveyed by persuasion and faithful action rather than subjugation; that people don't have to share your faith for you to love, respect, and work with them for the good of everyone; that a key purpose of faith is to make the world a better place for everyone, not just your group; that serving others and building up the community where you live is a holy calling; and that love is God's overarching purpose for life, then this book is for you.

The disavowal of power has had negative consequences for our clergy, congregations, communities, and nation—never mind the greater values

8. Rev. Mark Fraley, personal conversation and notes.

that our faiths wish to share with the world. By reframing and reclaiming power as good and necessary, the leadership of pastors, priests, and rabbis will be reinforced; congregations will be reinvigorated; our ministry to our communities will be more effective; and the nation's justly cynical view of faith institutions will be counterbalanced by a new and more faithful narrative of positive religious citizenship.

Most importantly, though, we will be living more fully into the values of our faith traditions and of the truest meaning of servant leadership.

Power versus Acedia

Power means simply "the ability to act." The pressing nature of the pandemic shook us loose from a tendency to inaction. But what causes that tendency to inaction?

Most clergy and parishioners believe that "servant ministry," based on "emptying oneself" of power, is morally superior to the self-serving pursuit of power exalted in some religious circles. As we all know, "power tends to corrupt, and absolute power corrupts absolutely." The pursuit of power is viewed as unseemly, inappropriate, and probably immoral. Many view power as demonic and in opposition to faith values.

This deep-set distrust of power is the spiritual malaise of acedia, one of the Seven Deadly Sins. Acedia is a broad-brush term that can embrace depression, laziness, uncertainty, feeling sorry for ourselves, helplessness, or what counselors call "stuckness." John Bunyan's *Pilgrim's Progress* speaks of the Slough of Despond, as if we are mired in a spiritual bog. Poet and spiritual writer Kathleen Norris observes that "the concept of acedia has always been closely linked with that of vocation."[9] "Acedia's genius," she writes, "is to seize us precisely where our hope lies, to tear away at the heart of who we are, to mock that which sustains us."[10] That in which we most believe seems the most impossible. It diminishes our worth by making us question the worth of what we are doing. Its practical result is inaction.

9. Norris, *Acedia*, 43.
10. Norris, *Acedia*, 44.

Reclaiming Power in Congregational and Community Ministry

Differentiation and Leadership

The spiritual opposite of acedia is zeal. Zeal is a bold, passionate commitment to act on what you believe. Unfortunately, in many congregations, zeal is considered a potentially uncontrollable fire that needs to be put out at once. Leaders worry about how other people feel, about going out on a limb, about taking a risk. In other words, they engage in fused or undifferentiated behavior. Ideally, leaders are differentiated, meaning that in their dealings with others they are clear about who they are, what they believe, and where they stand. In congregations, though, leaders often believe that to be undifferentiated—unable to set boundaries and over-sensitive to the desires and sensibilities of others—is what it means to be a community. They mistake undifferentiated behavior for unity and peacemaking. They think being undifferentiated means that they're practicing servant ministry.

Confusing servant ministry with undifferentiated behavior neuters leadership. As Ed Friedman taught us, differentiation is essential to leadership. While many qualities make a leader, the ability to stake out and stand up for a strongly held personal position is a baseline. A leader's differentiation will create tension and threaten the false unity of a system, but it also creates healthy differentiation further down the chain, opening the door for new ideas.

The Gift of Chaos

Septima Clarke, the iconic organizing strategist and trainer at the Highlander School, once said, "I have a great belief that whenever there is chaos, it creates wonderful thinking. I consider chaos a gift."[11] Leadership often emerges best in chaos. Chaos turns the status quo upside-down and forces people into differentiated positions. Normally, congregations believe that they are achieving unity and harmony when actually they are constantly trying to control their own thoughts and those of others to avoid any potential for conflict. Without the gift of chaos, most congregations can only be dragged into adaptive change kicking and screaming.

The chaos of the pandemic was an acceleration of the slow-moving storm front that has been consuming mainline congregations for fifty years. It forced us to discover our power to adapt when it's necessary. We should cultivate that power. It is the resource we need—have always needed—not

11. Ricks, *Waging a Good War*, 12.

only to survive but to thrive in the reality of post-faith America, a time when most Americans do not see the usefulness or relevance of religion anymore and even perceive it as a threat.

National distrust of religion can be traced back at least to 9/11, when grieving Americans came to our congregations the following weekend only to receive confused pablum. Our response to the pandemic presents a hopeful alternate narrative. Whereas on 9/11, we dropped the spiritual ball, many found their faith institutions to be a critical support during COVID. This even though we had to do many things that beforehand our congregants would have considered anathema, like drive-through communion, guitar-strumming outdoor worship, video services, and Zoom Bible studies. We have learned that the core of the message is what matters, not how it is conveyed. The core of the message has the power to change lives and the future. How do we continue to employ that power for the good of our congregations, communities, and world?

Post-COVID congregations must face the sparse return of the pandemic diaspora. Should we scramble to get them back into our sanctuaries? Give up on them and start recruiting new folks? Reimagine our ministries as more to a dispersed congregation with whom we remain in touch through creative use of technology? Downsize—get used to doing our ministries with fewer resources and a smaller core of dedicated people? Reimagine faith altogether? An argument can be made for trying all of them, probably all at once, but one thing is certain: Adaptation is key. To adapt, there needs to be leadership. That leadership needs to come both from clergy and their congregants. For leaders to lead, they must understand power. For power to be effective, it must be shared.

What Power Isn't in "the World Come of Age"

In a series of letters written from prison to his friend Eberhard Bethge from April 30 to August 3, 1944, theologian Dietrich Bonhoeffer developed the concepts of "the world come of age" and "religionless Christianity."[12] The world has grown up, Bonhoeffer argued, and no longer needs God and religion to find fulfillment, meaning and purpose. This creates a radical shift in the role of the church, which can no longer view itself as parent to a helpless child, a position which only encourages justified rejection and hostility from the capable adults it is attempting to dominate.

12. Barnett and Wojhoski, *Letters and Papers,* 364.

The church instead must be "religionless-worldly Christians . . . those who are called out, without understanding ourselves religiously as privileged, but instead seeing ourselves as belonging wholly to the world." The church "will have to confront the vices of hubris, the worship of power, envy, and illusionism as the roots of all evil."[13] It must stop trying "to prove to secure, contented, and happy human beings that they are really miserable and desperate" and "that [the world] cannot live without God as its guardian."[14]

Bonhoeffer has listed the misuses of power that religion must reject: privilege, arrogant superiority, elitism, condescension, overreach (hubris), envy (power hunger), illusionism (distracting the world from its real needs and strengths by sleight of hand), and "the worship of power," believing that dominating power is the end goal. Bonhoeffer accuses the Christian church of misusing power. It reads like a list of the qualities of today's partisan American Christianity, exactly what unifying faith must counteract. "The world come of age" is a prophetic distillation of our postmodern reality, in which younger generations no longer need religious faith to find meaning in their lives and question our relevance and positive influence on the world.

Bonhoeffer views "the world come of age" as a net positive for humanity and for religious faith. The God needed is humble and grounded in worldly reality. "To this extent, one may say that . . . the world's coming of age . . . has cleared the way by eliminating a false notion of God [and] frees us to see the God of the Bible, who gains ground and power in the world by being powerless."[15] "The world come of age," he argues, has humbled religion into its proper place, to bear witness to a servant God grounded in human experience.

"The church is only the church when it is there for others." Bonhoeffer imagines postmodern institutional religion shorn of the trappings of dominating power. "It must give away its property to those in need," good guidance to judicatories trying to figure out what to do with empty buildings! "The clergy must live solely on freewill offerings of the congregations and perhaps be engaged in some secular vocation," a prediction of bi-vocational ministry.

> The church must participate in the worldly tasks of life in the community—not *dominating* [italics mine] but helping and serving.
> It must tell people in every calling . . . what it means 'to be there

13. Barnett and Wojhoski, *Letters and Papers*, 503.

14. Barnett and Wojhoski, *Letters and Papers*, 26–27.

15. Barnett and Wojhoski, *Letters and Papers*, 480.

> for others' . . . It will have to see that it does not underestimate the
> significance of the human 'example' . . . the church's word gains
> weight and power not through concepts but by example.[16]

Bonhoeffer anticipates a postmodern religion sans property, presumed cultural importance and fulltime professional staff. Religious communities must instead lead by human *example* of God's people being "there for others." Again, he prophesies the age in which we live, where unifying congregations seek to better their local settings through service, mutuality, and cooperation. While he doesn't say this, he is laying groundwork for *democratized faith communities*, meaning that faithful believers, individually and corporately, take on the responsibility of being God's hands and feet in the world.

The Faith Communities Today report accents the importance of democratization and service to vital faith communities. Among the healthy traits it sees in thriving congregations are community engagement, diversity in the pews, "significant lay involvement, including contributing financially and volunteering" and congregants who "live out their faith commitments in everyday life and tell others about the congregation."[17]

Bonhoeffer's anticipation of bivocational clergy raises an issue which must be part of a discussion of the democratization of congregations. Clergy have been placed in an untenable position for decades, arguably centuries. Like the identified patient in a sick family system, they have become the "identified believers" in their congregations, called upon to do work that properly belongs to the congregants themselves. Pastor, priest, and rabbi are expected to be the living embodiment of the congregation.

This disempowers congregants and places too much power in the hands of clergy. It creates a potentially abusive cycle: either clergy misuse their power, or they are overwhelmed by the responsibility. The plethora of books, trainings, and resources, including this one, meant to shore up clergy's professionalism, self-care, and understanding of system dynamics are as much symptom as cure. The professional clergy is a holdover from the time that clergy played a uniquely sanctified role in the symbolic dynamics of faith. Seminaries train them for it; clergy, congregants, and judicatories expect it.

But in "the world come of age," "religionless-worldly" faith requires clergy to lay aside the trappings of sanctified priesthood and play a role more akin to a community organizer. This is especially vital now, as it becomes

16. Barnett and Wojhoski, *Letters and Papers*, 503–4.

17. Thumma, "Twenty Years of Congregational Change," 27.

harder for otherwise healthy congregations to afford full-time staff. The only way for many congregations to survive in these times is for their congregants to become less dependent on clergy and more dependent on their own God-given power. This book is intended to be a resource not only for clergy but for lay leaders seeking to empower themselves and their congregants.

The reality of smaller, poorer congregations, less institutional clout, fewer staff, justified cultural cynicism and the need for an alternative witness of community leadership emphasizing service, reconciliation, and "being there for others," requires the democratization of faith institutions, where the people in the pews take responsibility for implementing the mission of their congregations. But often our congregants (and clergy!) are disillusioned or poorly equipped to take on such responsibility. How can they recognize and implement the power they need to be faithful, responsible servants in these times?

We've talked about what power *isn't*. Now let's talk about what it *is*.

2

What Is Power?

Power I Didn't Know Existed

YEARS AGO, AT MY church in Fort Worth, Texas, there was a minor dispute between our church's council, the session, and the trustees, who are charged with the church trust, legal and property matters, and matters related to the church as a corporation in the state. The matter was over whether to sign a contract with particular stipulations. The session wanted it signed, but the trustees believed it was a bad contract.

Though I saw the trustees' point, I was frustrated. In the final analysis, under Presbyterian (USA) polity, they operate under the authority of the session and must do as bidden. I broached this with the president of the board of trustees and got a lesson in power.

"Bob, ultimately you have to do as the session says," I told him in an appropriately diplomatic voice.

"No, I do not." Bob was a retired lawyer who in his younger days had suffered death threats while investigating corruption. He always spoke slowly and considered his words carefully, even now when he was obviously incensed. "I don't have to do what the session tells me to do, and the trustees don't have to do what the session tells us to do. Not if we truly feel like it's the wrong course of action."

"But, Bob, how can you stand against the session? What can you do?"

"I am the president of the corporation. The vice president and treasurer of the corporation are also trustees. All we have to do is refuse to sign any document that the session puts in front of us."

"But then," I said, flummoxed, "all the session will do is disband the trustees and create a new board." But already I could see the problem. Bob put it in words:

"Do you seriously think that after all of that, you'd find nine qualified people to serve as trustees, out of whom even one would be willing to sign that contract?"

His point was clear. The session had the authority to override the trustees and if necessary, dissolve them, but the consequent fallout would be terribly damaging. No one qualified to serve as trustee would dare do so under those conditions. They'd likely be mad as hell.

The trustees had the session over a barrel. I suggested that Bob come to session, report the trustees' resistance, and help the session find an alternative. He did. The discussion was upbeat. A resolution to the impasse was easily found.

Bob was not engaged in a power play with the session. That was what he wanted to avoid. But to do that, he had to assert his and the trustees' power and demand the respect they were due. To think of the relationship of the trustees to the session simply from the perspective of the PCUSA Book of Order was to deny the trustees the respect they deserve and need to get their job done.

This was a healthy example of the natural dynamic of overt and covert power in congregations. Any pastor, priest, or rabbi can tell you there are "official" and "unofficial" power brokers in their congregation. Among the unofficial power brokers, though, are those who use their power in a healthy fashion and others who exert it in shadowy, manipulative, and self-serving ways. These latter thrive in the dark, and the darkest corner of any congregation's life is the concept of power itself. The fact that power is anathema in congregations makes it unspoken. The unspoken is the most powerful force in any organizational system. Those who use power manipulatively depend on our discomfort with it to keep their machinations hidden and their intentions clouded until they can achieve their goals.

Let's ask what might have happened had Bob been a meek little church mouse and abided by the ethic that all power is bad. He and the trustees might have said nothing and gone ahead with signing the documents. The church would then have been stuck with something the experts knew was a bad idea. Or, he might have decided to "speak truth to power" and told us what he thought, then gone ahead and signed against his better judgment.

Either way, the result would have been a bad decision that left undercurrents of resentment and disenfranchisement. It would have spread in whispers among the trustees' supporters and resulted in a rift. That rift could have manifested in many ways, such as ongoing tension between the session and trustees, overall distrust of the session and the pastor, or possibly a larger, more overt rift. Underground resentments can lead to churches splitting or pastors getting run out. There would probably have needed to be more than just that one bad decision—but decisions made in a disenfranchised way are rarely one-offs: They normally represent a larger systemic dysfunction.

This was headed off by a wise, worldly, and experienced church leader who knew that power matters as much in the church as it does in the real world; that power exercised poorly is as disastrous in the church as it is in the real world; and likewise, that power exercised well enables a congregation (or a community) to live into its better angels.

The Ability to Act

My understanding of power has been framed by my years in faith-based community organizing. I was first introduced to a fully formed concept of power at a Ten-Day Training sponsored by the Industrial Areas Foundation. There I was told that the term "power" comes from the Latin *posse*, which simply means "the ability to act." It is effectiveness.

At that conference, I heard nationally respected organizer, educator, and Roman Catholic Christian Ernesto Cortes give a presentation on two types of power. One type is *power over.* The other is *power with.* You could frame these two types of power, Ernie said, as *dominating power* and *the power of love.* "We are about the power of love," he said.

This is a dramatic reframing of power and its purpose. Power is a tool that can be used destructively or constructively, as self-serving or community-building, to dominate or to unite. Many religious people view power only as dominating power. It can be used positively by authorized people who embody the lordship of God on earth (bishops or other authority figures) or negatively by those who wish to impose their agenda in contrast to the will of God. Theologically this derives from and expresses an ancient view of God as a feudal suzerain whose dominion must be enforced or defended. This is an early biblical perspective, but it is highly problematic in democratic societies.

Unfortunately, this is the only perspective on power that many modern religious leaders, despite being steeped in the "servant leader" model, understand; and that most parishioners, who operate in the less forgiving "real" world, think is the effective way to accomplish things.

In my first church, one family's financial success played out as power in the church. They were the biggest donors and had funded some small building improvement projects. The family was insular. A common pattern is for insular families to build a power base in smaller congregations. This is a dynamic that clergy need to be aware of. The congregation becomes an extension of the family. A congregation is also an easy place to build power because church people are uncomfortable with it, so they are unable to resist unhealthy expressions of it.

The matriarch of this family was the church treasurer. She required me to come to her house every two weeks to receive my paycheck. While I was there, she would expound on everything that was wrong with the church and the world. I had no choice but to listen. I was enormously frustrated. I had thought my status as pastor would afford me some authority to resist this disempowering situation, but that wasn't the case. I knew the power dynamic was imbalanced. I knew she was playing, and winning, a power game. But I didn't have the skills or insight to respond. My limited understanding of power hamstrung me.

Since the only way I understood power was as dominating, and it was not in my nature to dominate, I didn't know what to do, so she walked all over me. Sometimes I would try to turn the tables, but these were awkward attempts at "reverse domination." All I did was embarrass myself, in the process shoring up her family's power even more. In the dominating power game, I would always be the loser.

Over time, the balance of power changed. Much of it came down to the simple practice of pastoring over a long period of time. I developed good relationships, significantly with the family most at odds with the treasurer's family. A Romeo and Juliet love story between children of those two families had a huge effect on the church's internal power dynamics. The matriarch was strongly against the lovers, forcing me to confront her and challenge her behavior. By then I was comfortable in my skin as the church's pastor; but in addition, I was respected and supported by the congregation. Over the natural course of things, *power with* had replaced *power over*. A lot had changed in the dynamics of the church, but most significantly for me, I now received my paycheck in my mailbox every two weeks!

There are times in congregational life, as well as in social justice matters, when dominating power needs to play a role. It is important to remember that there are just and appropriate uses of dominating power. But our intent, ultimately, is unifying power—power with—or as Ernie Cortes says, the power of love. And in the final analysis, power is a means, not an end. Its purpose is to get things done. Its purpose is effectiveness.

The Purpose of Power in Congregations

The single most important goal of a religious leader is to develop a congregation's power to be effective at its mission. While this is the goal of any leader, this is particularly incumbent on religious leaders because religious institutions are particularly obtuse about power and particularly bad at effectiveness.

Most congregational leaders can think of examples of our inability to do what we want to do. A common problem is developing a coordinated strategy for evangelism and welcoming new members. Some organizational genius will come up with a good plan that involves training an evangelism team, teaching ushers how to welcome visitors, and a communications strategy to stay in touch with visitors; then, after they're hooked, a way to welcome them into membership with mentoring, new member training, and so forth. A good faith effort is made to implement the plan. And then it eventually goes the way of all church plans. Not long after that, someone will say, "Why don't we come up with an evangelism and outreach plan?" and people will respond, "We tried that, and it didn't work!"

That statement, all too common in congregations, is the sad indication that people believe that nothing they do really works. "We have great worship, great children's programs, great community and world mission, but people still don't come. It just looks like nothing works."

Another level of challenge is community leadership. Often congregations and clergy try to engage faithfully to address matters of social justice, equity, and fairness in their local communities only to find themselves condescended to, outflanked, or ignored. Many faith organizations view social justice and positive community transformation as a part of their calling. But often such work seems Sisyphean, like the mythical Sisyphus, condemned to push a rock up a hill to the edge of a cliff in hopes of pushing it over, only to see it roll back down the hill and so be forced to start over, again and again for eternity.

This combination of past failure and the overwhelming nature of the work to be done can be debilitating and disheartening to congregations and their leaders. This is one reason that many faith communities focus on personal and corporate spiritual growth and not concrete, material change. Acedia is both the outgrowth and the cause of the over-spiritualizing of religious faith. We say churches should not be involved in the political/social realm at least partially because we feel like we are bad at it. We feel more comfortable in the spiritual realm, where it is nearly impossible to measure success or failure, than in the material, where winning and losing are quite concrete. Acedia takes root.

Strategically, to develop a congregation's power to be effective at its mission, leaders must

1. build up the leadership ability of their congregants;

2. create an atmosphere of shared power; and

3. lead the congregation to set winnable goals for itself at ascending levels of challenge.

This is not a step-by-step process but an ongoing and never-ending interplay of all three efforts.

Community organizing provides an effective way to understand this. For community organizers, their work operates in an eternal "now." Other than bettering their community in the most democratic fashion possible, they don't have long-term goals. Their issues emerge from the collective will of their constituents, whom they call leaders. Their ongoing, never-ending task is to train their constituents to be leaders who know how to organize their power to accomplish shared goals.

Congregations should operate in this regard the same way that community organizations do.

3

Framing, Reframing, and Power

ONE OF THE MOST important skills for leaders to have is the ability to re-frame—to see things from a different perspective and lead others to do the same. Bolman and Deal's revolutionary book *Reframing Organizations: Artistry, Choice, and Leadership* posits four frames through which to view organizational behavior. "A frame is a coherent set of ideas or beliefs forming a prism or lens that enables you to see and understand more clearly what's going on in the world around you," they write.[1] Leaders who understand these frames can find new ways to view power struggles, new avenues of ministry and effective ways to implement them.

The *structural* frame's metaphor is the factory. It looks at an organization mechanistically as a structure with clearly delineated rules, roles, responsibilities, rewards and punishments, products, and goals. The *human resource* frame uses the metaphor of the family and views organizations from the perspective of relationships between individuals, within groups, and among one another. The *political* frame's metaphor is the jungle. It views an organization from the perspective of competition and conflict.[2] Negotiation and power are key issues in the political frame. Finally, the *symbolic* frame, with the metaphor of the carnival or the temple, analyzes an organization from the perspective of meaning.[3]

1. Bolman and Deal, *Reframing Organizations*, 45.
2. Bolman and Deal, *Reframing Organizations*, 20.
3. Bolman and Deal, *Reframing Organizations*, 18.

In any situation, every single one of these frames is at play. Often when there is a conflict in which two sides are talking to cross purposes, it is because they are speaking from different frames. Likewise, when a given strategy doesn't work, it's likely because it didn't take each frame into consideration. A familiar example to faith organizations is developing a strategic plan with grand goals but not reflective of consensus (neglecting the political and human resource frames) or without benchmarks and metrics (disregarding the structural frame) or that takes a faith group in a radically different direction than it has perceived itself to be going (neglecting the symbolic frame).

Let's examine each of these frames from the perspective of congregations and power.

Power in the Structural Frame

The goal of the structural frame is to create an organization that runs well, properly balancing autonomy and interdependence, clarity of mission and creativity, freedom and structure, responsibility and initiative. Ideally, the organization works as smoothly as a well-oiled machine, and when it doesn't, the problems are easy to identify and fix.

The power of the structural frame lies in its ability to establish a clear mission, measurables to achieve that mission, and clear roles and expectations for everyone pursuing that mission. At a deeper level, though, structure plays a critical role in managing the most pervasive and destructive force in any congregation: anxiety. A good organizational system distributes conflict more evenly, rather than focusing it on an individual, and so relieves anxiety.[4] A good structure is "attuned . . . to task, technology, and environment."[5] Change is a challenge to any structure. For a structure to remain in place it must be adaptable. For leaders to lead well, they must be alert to changes that could require restructuring.

To recognize that structure manages anxiety explains not only why structure is essential, but why it responds to change so badly. People are used to the existing structure managing their systemic anxiety. Change stresses the system. Resistance results. The purpose of resistance is to maintain structure, or homeostasis, and stave off chaos. While that can be a problem when change is required, it's an understandable and generally

4. Friedman, *Generation to Generation*, 39.
5. Bolman and Deal, *Reframing Organizations*, 20.

healthy reaction, challenging us to be sure the change we are pursuing is the right path.

One way to understand faith communities is by their structure. Broadly speaking, three structures define how congregations operate: Episcopal, congregational, and Presbyterian. Each model is ancient. Each intends to give a faith group the power to do its mission. These structures also illustrate the promise and perils of any structural model, especially when it comes to facilitating shared power.

What Makes a Structure Work?

The power of any structure lies in its ability to mobilize people effectively toward an agreed goal. This means persuading them to go along with their model. This important detail is often missed when churches develop strategic plans. They imagine the new structure will solve all their problems. But the issue is: How do you get this congregation to take ownership of the strategic model you've developed?

There are four things required to make the structural model work: meaning and direction; how well it organizes people and resources to do the work required; reward and punishment; and trust. In an ideal company its employees are given a clear goal; an organizational arrangement that is clear and does its job well; pay hikes, perks, and promotions for rewards, and demotion, pay cuts, and firing for punishment; and a good relationship between management and employees that encourages both teamwork and independence, ensuring trust. When any one of these four fails or falls short, the power of the structural model is diminished.

It's common for people to assume that effectiveness is uniquely tied to structure. That is a dangerous mistake. To say anything has power is to say it is effective. All four frames—structural, human resources, political and symbolic—have great power. Believing that effectiveness rests particularly in the structural frame has been the downfall of many leaders.

Furthermore, the structural frame can be effective at something other than that for which it is intended. It may be terrible at organizing your congregation for mission but very effective at making your mission impossible. It may be useless for drawing in new members, despite its intent, but very good at enforcing strict rules that keep people in check and enacting the hidden agenda that the church remains unchanged. "There is no such thing as a dysfunctional organization," says Jeff Lawrence, "because every organization is perfectly aligned to achieve the results it gets."[6]

Structure is particularly good at maintaining the status quo, or homeostasis. But if the homeostasis needs to change, then examining not only how well it accomplishes the necessary tasks, but whether it provides meaning and direction and whether people truly trust it—the symbolic and human relations frames—is the best way to bring it about. The challenges the Roman Catholic Church faces illustrate this.

The Roman Catholic Church is an episcopally structured model. It is hierarchical, based on the monarchical style of government common in the period in which it was founded. Despite its worldwide and millennia-long impact, recently the Roman Catholic Church has been under assault in three key areas: meaning, rules, and trust.

Cases of sexual predation among Roman Catholic clergy and the revelation of decades of church cover-up have eroded trust and called the entire hierarchical model into question. The church is under pressure to form committees of non-clergy professionals—lawyers, doctors, police chiefs, psychologists and so on—to independently examine cases of sexual misconduct. These committees have no place in the structure of the Roman Catholic Church, which doesn't allow for lay leadership at any level; but pressure from furious church members and politicians, district attorneys, and the public in general, has already led to the formation of independent advisory boards.

The problem with the hierarchical structure is that it doesn't share power. It is the structural manifestation of dominating power. Dominating power only works as long as the dominated remain docile. In the age of democracy, dominating power needs to adapt. The Episcopal model is the least democratic of the three overarching congregational structures. Most episocopal-style denominations have adapted, counterbalancing hierarchy with democratic processes. The Roman Catholic Church has yet to do so in a substantive way.

Other episcopally-structured denominations have morphed, certainly in the United States, to reflect the more democratic leanings of its constituents. The Episcopal Church in America prides itself that its governance model reflects the structure of the United States government. Episcopally-structured denominations empower individual church boards, vestries

6. Heifetz et al., *Practice of Adaptive Leadership*, 17.

and committees to engage their non-clergy members. These actions have shored up trust in the hierarchy.

Dominating Power and Patriarchy

An experienced pastor who'd worked in smaller churches and for a decade at the conference level was encouraged by friends to apply for a "big steeple" position in her conference. She was very well qualified and had many strong references. After submitting her name to the bishop, for whom she worked directly, she heard nothing for several weeks, then he called her into his office. "I'm not submitting your name," he told her. "I don't think you have enough experience. I think you have two good jobs left in you. Take a small church for five years or so, then apply for this kind of position to complete your career." The pastor left the meeting feeling humiliated and certain that bishop's preference for male pastors had been the deciding factor. And of course, a man got the job.

Despite the increasing number of women in ministry, not to mention the fact that in most congregations, women outnumber men in the pews, religious institutions still have a long way to go before women are truly on an equal footing with men. Episcopally structured denominations are hardly the only culprits. Male dominance is taken for granted in more traditional or fundamentalist congregations and denominations, most of which are structured more in the congregational or the Presbyterian model.

Patriarchal church governance undermines shared power. Disempowering fully half of your congregants is an obvious expression of dominating power. Even if you have congregational or representative government, if you are also patriarchal you are practicing dominating power. Anything that creates "second-class congregants" is an expression of dominating power that will not serve our congregations well in this time when shared power is truly required. It is also nonadaptive behavior as our culture increasingly recognizes women's equality.

And it's not just women clerics who notice the problem; it is the women in the pews. Some female clergy interviewed for this book perceive a marked decrease in women's church attendance that they attribute to patriarchal attitudes.

Accountability and Managing Conflict

A new pastor arrived at a church only to be ambushed by a controversy surrounding the formation of the pastor search committee a year before. After the previous pastor left, a committee was formed to recommend candidates to search for the new pastor. The deliberations of this committee were to be frank and honest and therefore confidential. One financially well-off candidate who lobbied hard to be on the search committee was deemed unqualified. The committee, especially three women deacons, raised concerns about his controlling nature and his drinking.

Shockingly, another member of the committee was secretly recording the proceedings and played this recording to the candidate in question. The matter came to a head when the new pastor arrived.

One night in a drunken rage the failed candidate called all three of the women who had raised concerns about him. All three served on the church council. To two of them he spoke directly, cursing and belittling them. The third was not home so he left her a long voice message.

The first two women, ashamed and uncertain how to respond to his bullying, kept their silence until the third woman chose to play the recording of his call to the council.

The candidate's behavior was representative of a long-standing political problem of "official" versus "unofficial" systems in the church, but the council did not respond by burying the issue under the rug, as is often the case. They were outraged. They agreed that the proper response was public. The council must censure the offending candidate, who himself was a non-serving deacon. There was some concern about this, especially since the man's wife and mother, both members of the church, were deeply respected. But all agreed such bullying to serving deacons must not stand. At the council's request the pastor drafted a letter of censure but agreed to inform the offender's wife and mother of the decision before sending it.

When he spoke to the wife and mother, it was clear that they were in a deeply codependent relationship with the alcoholic offender. It had been his hope that they could be convinced to cooperate with the council to correct his behavior, but he was not surprised that this was not possible. The letter of censure was sent to the offender and placed in the public record of the council. The deacons were free to speak of it in the congregation to offset potential misinformation.

Creating accountability is one of the most important jobs of any structure. As was observed earlier, one of the main purposes of structure is to create an effective system of rewards and punishments that keep people on task. Many denominations continue to have rules and processes that enforce behavioral norms on pastors, congregations, and members. The Episcopal and Presbyterian models of government build in important levels of accountability. Congregants, boards, and pastors are accountable to a diocese, district, or presbytery. Inside a congregation, though, accountability can be trickier.

Structure and Anxiety

Within a given congregation, there is one issue that undermines structural power: volunteerism. Faith organizations have a small handful of employees whose job is to organize and incentivize an enormous group of volunteers. Without salaries, benefits, and other perks it is very hard to get anyone to do what you want them to do! One of the key components of structural power is seriously compromised by the fact that it is very difficult to come up with an effective reward and punishment system in a volunteer-based organization.

In the case above, the fact that there was a set denominational process for punishing the offender, censure, did not mean that the board would use that process. Many boards might have done nothing but bite their nails and hope for the best. The council members were not motivated by rules but by a strong moral commitment, already entrenched in the values of the church, to fairness and facing conflict in a direct fashion. In other words, the symbolic and political frames undergirded their structural response.

Individual congregations often do not give much thought to setting guardrails for conflict. This can play out most awkwardly in congregationally structured institutions that do not have a higher authority (other than God!) to which they are responsible.

A congregational church is for the most part autonomous. This entirely democratic organization is unwieldy when it comes to the four things that make the structural model work: meaning, organization, reward and punishment, and trust. Even if a large group of people by majority vote decides on meaning and reward and punishment, how does that group then keep itself on task and enforce their reward and punishment system? And what about the minority that voted against it? Are we going to operate by mob rule? Trust quickly fails in this kind of scenario. While I advocate democratization, one must recognize the challenges that attend it. Many of them occur when there is too much freedom and not enough structure.

Structure manages anxiety. Lots of congregations either don't consider structure very important or pay little attention to the structure they have developed. Manuals of operation remain unrevised for years. Not only that, but many congregations haven't updated their child protection, sexual harassment, and personnel policies, or even have them. These are matters of morality, justice, and legal protection. As painful and frustrating as it can be, blow the cobwebs off those notebooks and make sure you regularly update them. The whole purpose of structure is to make things easier. If the necessary work of the church is confusing, difficult, or unfair, your structure needs to be addressed.

Conflict is inevitable, no matter what your structure. But without structure, conflict, often pointless and personal, becomes the only outlet for congregational anxiety. The congregation's life can become consumed by power struggles and staffing and money issues.

In some churches, the chaos attendant to loose structure causes so much anxiety that people give their power away to someone who is only too glad to have it. In congregational churches that do not have an overarching judicatory to hold the congregation and clergy accountable, the risk is that power is given to someone who abuses it. It is quite common to see charismatic, authoritarian clergy rise to dominance in such churches. In more extreme situations, this can become cultic, with the leader defining the mission and doling out reward and punishment by his own lights, reinforced by the blind trust of the congregation.

Authoritarian leadership is hardly limited to congregational churches. Many congregations, regardless of affiliation, cede far too much power to the clergy. One Presbyterian church's council had relaxed its leadership responsibility when for more than a decade its pastor had, for all intents and purposes, done their job for them in a way that pleased them. When they hired their next pastor, they looked for that same sort of authoritative leadership. This time the pastor was imperious, narcissistic, and deeply insensitive. He mismanaged finances and alienated members, all while telling the session that they were not in charge, he was. Finally, they asserted leadership and the pastor left by mutual agreement, but a lot of damage had been done.

Leaders, above all, both clergy and lay, must be wedded to their structural responsibilities, or things will quickly descend either into chaos or autocracy.

Of course, congregational leaders can take their jobs too seriously, as well, hounding one pastor after another out of office or constantly engaged in infighting (power struggle) that undermines any sense of shared mission. In these cases, the structure has lost track of the symbolic frame that gives it meaning and purpose. It has become mired in politics unmoored to meaning and driven by anxiety.

Closed Systems

Many churches operate as congregational churches even if they are not technically congregational. They want autonomy from larger structures, often for unhealthy reasons. A serious risk is that such a congregation becomes a closed system. While all organizations have aspects of both closed and open systems, in an unhealthy closed system people have subsumed their individual identity into the group, resulting in unhealthy and exclusive dynamics. They are characterized by "intrapsychic rigidity" and resistance to change. They "treat the present as though it were the past."[7] The dynamics are like a family system dealing with incest, alcoholism, or some other dark secret.

A church doesn't need to be congregational in structure to be a closed system, but any church that is a closed system wants to become congregational as quickly as it can. It doesn't want an outsider to upset its unhealthy dynamic or expose its dread secret.

And the cleric is an outsider.

One pastor discovered this the hard way. His church was a long-time closed system. His attempts to open the church to new members and to address its secrets and hidden cruelties—and to involve the larger regional body in the process—only brought trouble on him and his family. Though many in the church supported him, they were so cowed by the system that they saw him and the judicatory, rather than the church's power-mongers, as the problem.

The Challenge of Compromise

For several years I served on a board responsible for distributing federal funding to local homelessness and housing providers. The board comprised

7. Nichols and Schwartz, *Family Therapy*, 532.

at least thirty representatives and served two counties that included a major metroplex and a vibrant small city. The purpose of the board was to distribute funding, coordinate work, and make sure every voice was heard.

Those voices were often a cacophony. At the table were politicians from two city and two county governments, local government housing agencies, nonprofits providing various services, and religiously affiliated homeless ministries. All were vying for a limited pot of money. Not everyone could get what they wanted. People could become bitter, angry, suspicious and accusatory. But money got distributed and services got provided.

Representative decision-making matters when your goal is shared power. It is neither possible nor practical for everyone to be at the table for every decision. Still, as many points of view as possible need to be represented for the decision to have any validity.

Representation is messy. Family court judges say that in criminal court, you see the worst people on their best behavior; but in family court you see the best people on their worst behavior. Many board meetings are like family court!

In many congregations, though, especially smaller ones, the pendulum swings the other way. Leaders are so willing to avoid conflict that they put off or make unconsidered decisions. Leaders adapt to weakness: They choose the path that will hurt the least feelings, believing they are empathetic or that they are avoiding conflict. How many times have we heard, or said, "I'd have supported a controversial position, but I had to think about how other people feel?"

Friedman says that "empathy has become a power tool in the hands of the weak to sabotage the strong."[8] Worried about stepping on toes, leaders are driven by anxiety and take the path of least resistance. Many polities emphasize that leaders are to seek God's will, which is not always the will of the majority. But this transcendent understanding of what leadership means gets lost in the mistaken notion that leadership means ruffling the least feathers.

In contrast, the homeless board on which I served was full of vibrant, distinctive personalities who did not hesitate to lay their interests on the table and defend them to the death. Especially when it came to distribution of resources, things got heated. If one believes that decisions should be made without conflict, it might seem chaotic. But with strongly differentiated leaders, conflict over important decisions is inevitable.

8. Friedman, *Failure of Nerve*, 26–27.

But decisions were made. Resources were distributed. Most interested parties returned to the table to find ways to work together even if they didn't get what they wanted. Those who didn't get the funding they wanted went back to reassess their programming to see how they could improve to meet the performance standards of the federal grants. Overall, homeless services continued to improve.

The Presbyterian Church (USA)'s decades-long controversies regarding LGBTQ inclusion presents some important lessons about representation.

Structures Exist to Preserve Themselves

In 1996, the PCUSA enacted a rule that would disallow the ordination of anyone in a sexual relationship outside of the marriage between a man and a woman. The rule was approved by the General Assembly and most regional judicatories (presbyteries).

This rule targeted mainly LGBTQ individuals but had a shotgun effect hitting a far wider field, such as single people actively dating or people living together but unmarried. Since the PCUSA ordains elders and deacons as well as clergy, this was a ban affecting laity as well as pastors.

Many congregations resisted this rule. Presbyteries, to whom clergy and churches are accountable, responded in different ways. In some cases, congregations and clergy were prosecuted and punished; in others, resistance was ignored or even encouraged. In either case, systemic behavior had a human cost. If a presbytery actively enforced the rule, certain lay people could not be ordained, causing alienation. Clergy could lose their jobs and even their ordination.

Likewise, if clergy, a church, or a presbytery chose to ignore or resist the rule, congregations (or individuals) could press charges against them, leading to prosecution.

Every structure exists to preserve itself and serve its own interests and not the needs and interests of the individual—often at cost to the individual. The reason that ecclesiastical structures are under pressure today is the rise of individualism. Individuals have both real and perceived power and autonomy in the modern world. In contrast, structures exist to organize the power of groups of people toward shared goals. That means that some people don't get what they want.

In 2012, after sixteen years of tension, the General Assembly overturned the 1996 rule, replacing it with a "live and let live" rule that each council could make its own decisions about whom it allowed in ordained service. Once again, this was approved by most presbyteries. This illustrates one of the more interesting aspects of representative government: changing moods and mores can overturn established rules and structures, often within a generation or less. Representative government depends on this reality. Those who resist the status quo can fight on, hoping that eventually they will overcome. Those in favor of a controversial status quo can hope that gradually a "slippery slope" will develop. As more people come to accept and live with it, the status quo will become a commonplace. Time is on the side of those who promote change.

What Happens When You Lose?

This majority decision for inclusion did not represent the will of a powerful minority. The decision has precipitated a massive split. At this writing, the PCUSA has experienced a 28 percent membership decline since the 2012 GA decision.[9] By comparison, over twenty years, mainline protestants have declined by 12.5 percent.[10] Many of the churches leaving the denomination are "big steeple" churches with large membership bases, big-name pastors, and a great deal of money. Their departure has had a serious negative impact on the national and structural power of the PCUSA.

When people do not feel represented, the losers may well pick up their toys and leave. They can, after all, form a new structure that represents *them*! Representative government's power depends on keeping as many parties as possible if not happy, at least not too disgruntled. It is a balancing act between "top down" and "bottom up" leadership and constituencies with varied interests, needs and resources. The attempt to balance competing interests leads some people to frustration that can boil over into schism.

Many resource-rich churches have departed the PCUSA to join or form denominations that are representative of their interests. In the process they have depleted the resources of the PCUSA. The hope is that changing moods and mores will ultimately work in our favor and that our moral commitment to inclusion will result in more members and resources. We can take comfort that we are on the right side of history. But in the immediate future, the depletion of our resources, both members and money, is a crisis.

9. Comparison based on PCUSA statistics: Presbyterian Church (USA), "2012 Summaries of Statistics; Presbyterian Church (USA), "2021 Comparative Summaries."

10. Thumma, "Twenty Years of Congregational Change," 13.

The Strengths and Limitations of Structural Power

The story of Bob, the president of the trustees who successfully defied the church board, illustrates the limitations of structural power. Structures can attribute power to individuals and councils. They can provide the ability to enforce that power. But there are many other avenues of power, and structural power is the weakest of them all. Bolman and Deal's remaining three frames —human resource/relationship, politics, and symbolism—all have power that outweighs structure. This is especially true for faith institutions that are minimally hierarchical. In such institutions the power of enforcement is negligible. Furthermore, to the extent that structures practice enforcement—i.e., excommunication, overzealous judicial commissions, etc.—the efforts are more likely to undermine rather than build trust. Persuasion, cooperation, and compromise are the best tools for resolving difficulties. These operate in the human resource and political frames.

Structural power ultimately is created. It is artificial. Real power ultimately comes from other sources.

However, structural power is essential. Without structure, organizations are riven by anxiety and descend into chaos and confusion. Structures organize people and resources to accomplish their goals effectively. A good structure is an essential tool for any organization to accomplish its mission. No organization can exist without some form of structure and the better the structure the more effective an organization is at accomplishing its mission.

How This Impacts Your Congregational Structure

A few key lessons from the above directly impact your own structure and planning.

a. *Structure manages anxiety.* Updating long-neglected policies is hard work. It forces your board to think about how well they are accomplishing the mission they have set for themselves and to reconsider whether "the way we've always done it" is really the best way. One way to judge that is simply, how anxious do people get when they need to figure out how to do certain things? Is it impossible to find someone to run the annual giving campaign? Does the campaign never raise nearly enough money? When the boiler breaks down, how does it get fixed? Is it always the same person who runs the sound system every

Sunday and things go south when they're away? If people are stressed about it, the structure is failing in ways that need to be addressed.

b. *Four qualities undergird structure: clarity of mission, good organization, a system of rewards and punishments, and the trust of its constituents.* This is why good strategic planning always starts with mission, the symbolic frame, and extrapolates out from there. Since most internal congregational dynamics can only enforce reward and punishment by the collective moral force of the people, the most important work a strategic planning team needs to do is to develop trust and buy-in and encourage shared ministry. We will deal with that more in the human resources frame. In your planning, use focus groups to sharpen your sense of mission and to determine what the problem areas are and what possible solutions people see. Regularly report back to them on your progress to make sure they continue to buy into what you're doing. Conscious effort must be put into making sure every group is represented and every voice is heard.

The most common structural complaint in any congregation is poor communication. While there's always someone who didn't get the memo, don't let it be because you didn't send it. The more open you are about your planning process, the more invested people will feel in the outcome. You will create a feedback loop where you tell them what you're doing and they tell you what they think about it, enabling you to hone your structure. Your priority is to build a structure that is trustworthy, and in which members feel invested.

c. *Your structure must be built on shared power.* This is not only moral, it is practical. The structure needs to engage as many people as possible in the work of the congregation. That means working committees, a method for engaging volunteers and recruiting new people onto ministry teams, figuring out how to train leaders, and promoting authorship, all of which will be addressed below.

d. *Put thought into how you will manage conflict.* Conflict is inevitable. Every congregation has its own method for dealing with it. A strategic planning team needs to examine how effective their church's conflict management style is. The most important thing to keep in mind is to minimize reactivity and promote deliberation and openness. Think about how to make sure that all players in a conflict feel respected and heard.

Often there is a particular person whose reactivity needs to be addressed and neutralized. There are some pastors or staffers whose natural fallback is reactive or even abusive behavior. Personnel committees and the board must be empowered and emboldened to address these behaviors. Even if it's not a problem now, it's good to prepare for it.

Lay leaders can also create or promote conflict. In most cases, the solution to every problem lies with a board that isn't afraid to step up either to hear both sides of a conflict and make a decision around it (if needed) or to address inappropriate behavior in staff or members. They need to be aware that it's a part of their responsibility that can't be avoided.

e. *Leaders must be fully invested in the plan.* Your board and staff shouldn't just rubber-stamp a plan. They are the ones who will be implementing it and evaluating it along the way. It is not uncommon for congregational boards and staff members to leave the strategic planning to the planning team and give it little thought beyond that. They must be directly involved in every aspect of the plan. The most vulnerable point in strategic planning is after the committee has handed the plan over to the board and staff, because there's a good chance they won't implement it.

With that in mind, it's vital to hear from staff and leaders what they need from a plan to make it as easy as possible to implement. A good plan will include, for instance, measurables and a process for evaluation and reconsideration as the plan moves forward. It will make it clear how it is to be implemented. Roles will be defined clearly so that you haven't given anyone too much (or not enough) to handle. All that needs to be developed with full input from leaders and staff.

Power in the Human Resources Frame

As pastor of a small church outside of Washington, DC, I faced a generational challenge common in the early 2000s. When I arrived, most of the congregation and its leaders were from "the Greatest Generation" who came of age during World War II. During my tenure there, we started to get many new and younger members, two or more generations behind the present leadership. Many of the older members expressed exhaustion and a desire to retire from their volunteer labor. To top it off we saw an unusual and upsetting number of deaths. Many of the best, most motivated leaders and volunteers succumbed to their age.

It seemed like a good time to restructure the church to allow older members to train newer members into leadership. I'd been pastor there for five years and felt I had developed the trust needed to lead change. Working with a church organization professional, we developed a plan for shared leadership between older and newer leaders with a transition process built in. Established leaders developed notebooks and disks of information to pass on. There was a process for assimilation and transition. We developed the plan with input from everyone, with the understanding that the goal was shared leadership that allowed exhausted leaders to step back and empower new leaders, while furthering the mission and traditions of the church as the earlier generation understood them, but in newer directions.

The training event for the new plan was attended by both newer and older members. To my surprise and horror, one of the older members most vociferous about wanting to retire from leadership, Mary Ann, stood up holding her committee notebook and said, "If you want to force me out of leadership, fine. I quit. Give it to someone else." She turned to her stunned younger counterpart whom she was supposed to mentor and handed her the notebook. "It's yours now."

The training was basically over at that point. So was the plan. Ultimately so was my ministry there. Several factors had led to this.

Power and Trust

For the previous five years, I had led the congregation to be more engaged in community organizing and social justice issues. This had been enthusiastically supported by many older parishioners, civic-minded members of the GI Generation, who remembered the days when the church had been active in the Civil Rights Movement. This renewed activism had led many younger people to the church.

But the terrible spate of deaths had decimated the older activist group, leaving members of the more cautious Silent Generation in leadership. They eschewed the risk-taking behaviors of the generation before them.

Excited as I was by the more social justice-oriented agenda I was pursuing with the younger members, I had missed the change in attitude among key leaders.

Nor had I fully appreciated the implications of the generation gap in my congregation. I knew that the younger and older members didn't know one another. I wanted to use the transition plan as a means for the younger and older generations to get acquainted. This was a mistake. I should have worked on building community first—the human relations frame. The leadership challenge should have been secondary. But I was in a hurry.

Finally, by this point in my ministry I should have been able to recognize that what people say is not always what they mean. Though some of the older members expressed how tired they were of leadership, *that did not mean that they were tired of power*. The feeling of ownership among long-term members of any organization runs deep. Despite themselves, and especially in a situation of a vast generational gap, the tendency to be a closed system, a church just for us, is very strong. Mary Ann may not have realized until that very moment how possessive she was of the church and how much she resented these whippersnappers (and this pastor) for trying to take away her power of ownership.

My brilliant structure was doomed to fail. Neither shared sense of mission nor trust had been adequately considered. The older and younger generations had different mission goals for the church. Trust in the plan was irrelevant. The congregation did not trust one another. Established members thought young people and the pastor were trying to wrest power from them. Younger people, and I, thought older people were holding on to power to the detriment of the church. Both sides were right!

The issue was power and who had it. My plan had viewed power-sharing as incidental to the goal of restructuring the church toward a certain vision. *Power-sharing, which I now recognize as one of the main goals for congregational success, cannot happen without establishing a baseline of trust.*

Trust falls into the human resources frame, which looks at organizations from the perspective of relationships and human growth and development. Its metaphor is the family. The family dynamic is present in all forms of congregations (indeed all organizations), large or small, but is especially pronounced in smaller churches (congregations of 200 or less). In these congregations, the family dynamic is so powerful that it can stymie growth. In the case study above, the established congregants viewed the newcomers as interlopers. They viewed the church as taking care of their "church family," which did not include the newer folks.

The Human Factor

There is a relationship between the human resources and political frames because both deal with people. One can easily transmogrify into the other and people can move easily between one frame and the other. In the case study above, established members came to view themselves from the human resources frame and the "others," and the pastor, from the political frame.

The human resources frame has enormous power. It is evident in the way we commonly speak of churches as "families." We mean this in a positive way: we are close to one another, we can depend on one another, this place is our home. At their best, congregations can accept one another's differences and find ways to connect that might mystify outsiders.

But families have problems. Both families and congregations can be open or closed systems, but no system is fully one or the other. No matter how open a family is, it is still exclusive. A congregation that calls itself a "family" can give the impression that visitors are not welcome. Families have habits, traditions, and ways of organizing themselves, conscious and unconscious norms uniquely theirs. Pastors joke painfully about the potential new member who is chastised for putting the Tupperware on the wrong shelf in the church kitchen. Strangers don't know those norms and may only discover them in awkward and embarrassing ways that make them feel inferior and unwelcome. Congregations often don't realize that they have these norms or how alienating they can be. These unwritten "family rules" can be a hindrance to congregational growth both numerically and spiritually.

The family dynamic can be a powerful force that makes the transition stage between a shepherding-size church (50 to 150 attending) and a programmed-size church (150 to 350 attending) extremely difficult to bridge. Congregations will say they want to grow to the next level, but the unconscious desire to maintain the family dynamic of a shepherding-size church will stall or reverse attempts to draw new members, develop new programs, or free the pastor or rabbi from the distractions of intense interpersonal dynamics.

This can also happen in reverse. A common dynamic for mainline churches is ongoing decline from a corporation- or programmed-size church toward a shepherding-size church. As this process takes place, long-term members increasingly identify themselves and their core as a family and become symbolically aligned with a congregational identity that is no longer relevant. They become "aristocratic" churches, a dangerous stage of congregational decline in which the congregation convinces itself that it occupies an elite status that must be preserved at all costs. Unless this dynamic can be overcome, such a congregation is on the fast track to closing altogether.[11]

Sometimes clergy in shepherding-size congregations are resistant to change because they feel more comfortable with the human, less organizational focus or because they like being the center of attention. Often a congregation becomes a substitute family for clergy. It is important for clergy to acknowledge their own investment in the congregation's status quo.

There is nothing wrong with a family dynamic in a congregation. The problem comes when the system cannot accommodate change. If a congregation cannot assimilate new members or new ideas, it will decline.

The Difference Between "Power Over" and "Power With"

Several years ago, Fort Worth's transportation authority, the T, changed a long-standing policy that had allowed the unhoused and poor to ride buses all day for free with a bus pass. Passes had been distributed among providers and clergy and were thus liberally distributed to people in need.

When the T decided to change the policy, there was immediate pushback from the faith community and from providers. In response, the T decided they would offer free two-hour passes. Providers were outraged. Two hours was how long it might take to get to a doctor's appointment or to your case worker or a job interview—never mind how you'd get back home once you got there or any other errands you needed to run.

The faith community organized a massive attempt to change the policy. No matter whom we talked to, however, or how many we turned out, it seemed that, if anything, the powers that be became more entrenched. What was really bewildering was that, as chair of the homeless coalition board, I was in two meetings, one with a city councilperson and one with the county executive, where we were accused of "bullying" the executive director of the T who had initiated the policy! No one had attacked him personally; there were no sit-ins in his office or around his house. Everything happened at public meetings. Most of us never even saw him. How could a man known to have initiated this policy in three other cities before Fort Worth, feel "bullied," and why in the world would politicians line up to protect him like a pride of lions protecting a cub?

---

11. Galindo, *Hidden Lives*, 73.

I can see only one logical conclusion. The board, its director, and city and county politicians thought they had already conceded to our demands when they authorized the two-hour pass. They thought they'd done us a favor! They didn't understand why we weren't grateful.

What they didn't understand is that *we were not satisfied because we were not involved.*

Bolman and Deal address the ineffectiveness of top-down decision-making. In one analysis, administrators in local school districts who developed plans to use government grants consistently ran into entrenched intransigence when "teachers greeted the news with resistance, criticism, and anger" because "the administration had committed to a new teaching approach without faculty input."

> The usual mistake is assuming that the right idea (as perceived by the idea's champions) and legitimate authority ensure success. This assumption neglects the agendas and power of the "lowerarchy"— partisans and groups in mid-level and lower-level positions, who devise creative and maddening ways to resist, divert, undermine, ignore, or overthrow innovative plans.[12]

This is the difference between *power over* and *power with*. The T thought they were conceding to public pressure with the two-hour pass. But top-down decisions are rarely respectful. They imply a paternalistic attitude that engenders resentment, undermines relationships by suggesting "we don't need to talk to you," and illustrates that other people's fate rests in your hands. A beneficent absolute ruler is still an absolute ruler. The people are disempowered.

Power with, in contrast, is built on relationships of mutual respect, equality, and shared investment in the community. It recognizes the power of the people and that the strongest policies are built on the often-frustrating process of conflict, dialogue, understanding, and negotiation.

With shared power as our goal and our means, then the challenge of volunteerism, which has been identified as a strain on the structural frame, may be addressed by good use of the human relations frame. We cannot *make* people do the work of the congregation, but they can be *inspired* to do it if they feel empowered and appreciated.

A key aspect of power is organizing people. Human relations in a church certainly depend on pastoral care, but leadership in the human relations frame is more than empathy, it is empowerment. How do we organize

12. Bolman and Deal, *Reframing Organizations*, 232–33.

people to work together, face and resolve differences, take on challenges and overcome obstacles with a sense of shared community and purpose? How do we organize people to do the work of God in their congregation, community, and world?

This is not simply a functional question. In a faith community, it is a spiritual question.

The Spirituality of Community

A woman regularly attended my church for years but never joined. She was a leader in mission and outreach and a dedicated member of the choir. Most people had no idea she wasn't a member. They loved her and she obviously loved them.

When I asked her why she never joined, she said it was because she didn't see herself as a Christian. "I just don't believe what the church believes," she said honestly.

I was struck by the fact that despite saying she didn't believe, she came forward for communion on Sunday, the most significant symbolic faith event in any church. "What does communion mean to you?" I asked her once.

She looked around and indicated all the people standing around. "This," she said. "These people."

She was testifying to the spiritual power of community.

The spiritual health of a congregation can be best measured by how well their sense of shared mission and purpose results in working together toward concrete goals within and beyond the four walls of church or synagogue. Recognition of the unique spiritual benefit of community life pushes back against the prevalent notion of individual spirituality that has dominated American religious culture for a century. In the past, there's been an assumption that faith communities fuel their parishioners individually to do good the rest of the week. Add to this the prevalence of self-help books and individualized religious views and practices. None of that is bad, but it is not enough. This individualized compartmentalization of spirituality contributes to the fragmentation of society. It creates a profound sense of loneliness.

Since World War II, massive demographic changes have so uprooted people that it is hard to find any place other than some small towns where there is a transcendent sense of togetherness. Congregations may be the last places left in American life where community remains a value—where people feel connected to one another despite age, race, social standing, individual identity, or political allegiance. Of course, congregations are just as susceptible to any of these divisions.

To live and act as a community with a distinct identity is a countercultural value. If our goal is shared power, the formation of community is essential.

A Distinctive Community

To focus on congregations as communities with distinct values and practices reframes us not only as a community that is sent out into the world, but also as one that gathers, supports, and builds one another up. This community spirit is an essential manifestation of the human resources frame. *A key task of faith leaders is to build an identity of distinctive values, practices, and character within their faith communities.* Many nondenominational churches and Ultra-Orthodox synagogues have developed distinctive identities in their faith communities, albeit in a negative way. Their message is "It's us against the world." This message has fueled America's culture war and caused the megachurch boom.

We need not view ourselves as at war with the world to build a unique community identity. Churches and synagogues already engage in distinctive practices and teach countercultural values. Our symbols give us character and purpose. We regularly practice worship, try not to divide ourselves according to cultural distinctions like political affiliation and socio-economic status, and teach radical things like "love thy neighbor."

What is needed is a conscious sense that everyone in this fellowship shares a distinct and unique identity that we value, unites us as a body, makes us different from the rest of the world, and to which we bear witness as a gift to the world; and that we're all in it together. A worshiping community is not a refueling stop for individuals who go back out and try to change the world one person at a time, but a gathered community with shared values and a corporate identity, who know that when we gather, we are truly whole, and when we work together, we are more powerful than if we are on alone. Indeed, to be good persons requires a community. "Our capacity to be virtuous depends on the existence of communities that have been formed by narratives faithful to the character of reality," writes Stanley Hauerwas.[13]

13. Hauerwas, *Community*, 116.

Church historian Diana Butler Bass says that the congregations doing best are engaged in intentional practice, meaning that they build their identity on distinctive disciplines, rooted in their faith tradition (as opposed to cultural or other practices), around which the congregation organizes itself. Such congregations may not be as big as others, but they reinforce the sense that to be people of faith is unique and grounded in a spiritual purpose. Such congregations

> construct faith as a way of life in community . . . distance themselves from surrounding values and self-describe in more theological, sacramental, mythical and mystical terms . . . and emphasize creativity and community more than organization and program.[14]

My Texas church emphasized Christian hospitality, homeless outreach, and traditional liturgy, including such spiritual practices as Vespers, Evensong, labyrinth walks, and deeply moving Passion Week services. These practices made us distinct from other programmed-size churches in the community. They drew people who were specifically interested in those practices and created a sense of vitality and community identity that sustained us when other similar congregations were struggling.

The Beloved Community

The formation of community has risks. Closed systems get that way because the participants believe they are expressing their community identity. Contrasting this is Martin Luther King's concept of the Beloved Community. The Beloved Community is a radically open society. As he describes it:

> We are tied together in the single garment of destiny, caught in an inescapable network of mutuality. And whatever affects one affects all indirectly. For some strange reason I can never be what I ought to be until you are what you ought to be. And you can never be what you ought to be until I am what I ought to be. This is the way God's universe is made; this is the way it is structured.[15]

For King, "the Beloved Community is seen to comprise the social condition of all human beings living together in an interdependent and interrelated whole created by the presence of love in human society."[16] The purpose

14. Butler Bass, *Practicing Community*, 18.

15. King, "Remaining Awake," 269.

16. Bridges, *Resurrection Song*, 168.

of pursuing integration, King said, was "to foster and create the 'beloved community' in America. . . . Our ultimate goal is genuine interfaith and intergroup living."[17] The Beloved Community is an essential counter to radical individualism, which King believed to be inadequate for the challenges of the modern world.

> No individual can live alone, no nation can live alone, and anyone who feels he can live alone is sleeping through a revolution. The world in which we live is geographically one. The challenge we face today is to make it one in terms of brotherhood.[18]

The concept of the Beloved Community is a beautiful metaphor and hence belongs in the symbolic frame; but for our present purposes, it has practical implications for how the human resources frame is implemented in a faith community. Such a community is open and hospitable, glad to welcome people from a variety of backgrounds. It practices forgiveness and reconciliation. Its goal is peace and wholeness for its community and world and respect for each person. It tries to be in microcosm what it aims for in macrocosm. Beyond itself, it seeks justice, fairness, and well-being for society writ large. It respects suffering and is willing to make corporate sacrifices for the sake of its greater values. It seeks to live as if the reign of God is a present reality in its day-to-day life.

This is a lofty, perhaps unreachable goal. But as a vision to drive organizing in congregations and beyond, it is inspiring and aspirational. A community that pursues this vision can foster bonds of trust that create mutuality and accountability and transcend and resolve differences. Because it appreciates suffering, it is also willing to take risks. Pursuit of the Beloved Community drives unifying congregations.

Anxious Power

A young Baptist pastor, a recent seminary graduate, was called to serve a shepherding-size (attendance around one hundred) rural southern congregation. The congregation had recently experienced a spate of thirty deaths that left them reeling. The pastor was told that the leadership wanted to grow the congregation. With that in mind, he began to recruit students

17. Bridges, *Resurrection Song*, 167.
18. King, "Remaining Awake," 268.

from the local Baptist college campus. Soon attendance was boosted almost to the number that had been lost in the recent deaths.

After eighteen months of ministry, the pastor received a vote of "no confidence" and was asked to leave.

Reflecting on the experience, the pastor says his mistake was not addressing the "angst and woes" of the congregation before he did anything else. "I should have spent time the first year not trying to cast the vision but trying to listen to history" and to the voices of those who'd lost loved ones. "These are the first matters to address," he said. He should have said from the pulpit, "This church is hurting. The last twelve years have been stupid hard in ways we may not have words for."

This neglect of the human dimension created what the pastor, Dustin Bannister, now a church and systems dynamics professional, calls "anxious power." The congregation felt in its bones that the church was not addressing their most profound need. "Every one of those empty pews has stories," he said. When the bereaved saw new people, often very different in age or race, sitting in their lost loved ones' pews, it increased their anxiety and sense of loss. Perhaps they'd imagined that "growing the church" would ease their grief. In fact, it made it worse.

When the pastor was fired, it was an expression of "anxious power," he says, but he doesn't hold it against them. They weren't pursuing power; they just "didn't want to hurt anymore." These folks, who had no power in any other aspect of their lives, recognized they had power in the church because of their tenure and the office they held. "They recognized they had some tool or skill to lessen that angst," and used that to eliminate what they thought was the cause of it: him.

In this case, structural power—the board's authority to speak on behalf of the church and to hire and fire—was used the way that one might take some anxiety pills one finds in the bathroom cabinet to ease stress. Structural solutions are like prescriptions. They only work if they are tailored to address a proper diagnosis. Without analysis of the human, political and symbolic issues underlying the congregation's malaise, structural solutions only provide a short-term fix, and may even become habit-forming. The pastor points out that between his firing in 2017 and 2020, the church hired and fired four pastors. Firing had become an addiction.

Congregations are crucibles of anxiety. We often join or create them out of anxiety, become anxiously dependent on them, and are wracked with anxiety should change occur. This anxiety creates power. It is the most powerful force in a congregation and needs to be understood and addressed before pursuing any other goals.

Every congregation's anxiety takes a different form. Clergy are wise to take the time to discern and understand what it is that the congregation most fears before attempting to make changes. Our larger goals need to be placed on the backburner until this very human dimension is properly addressed.

A new bishop and his associate arrived in a diocese recently riven by a denominational split. The first diocesan meeting they attended was rife with recriminations, accusations and personal attacks directed at one another and the new staff they'd only just met.

The associate bishop, stunned by the emotional barrage she'd just experienced, suggested to the bishop he use his power to "tell people no. This is not acceptable. You may not treat other people this way."

"I can do that," he replied. "I have the power to do that. But what I cannot do, what I do not have the power to do, is to create change. We have to get people to police each other and themselves. We have to get people to choose to treat each other well, or this will never change."

Change came over the course of two years, beginning with a behavioral covenant among diocesan leadership that created a sense of safety. People who feel they are being attacked will respond in kind; the covenant removed a key source of conflict.

Of course, some people viewed the covenant as an implicit attack on their behavior, compelling them to leave. These were the instigators—people for whom the prevailing atmosphere of anxiety created an opportunity to accrue anxious power. By reducing a key cause of anxiety, their power was taken away. Apparently, they did not understand or could not abide shared power.

Note how structural power was used in this situation. Structure manages anxiety, but it is heavily dependent on which of the other frames it is based upon. The structural power of the bishop, the political frame, was of no help. He could give an order but didn't have the power to change people or dynamics.

A written behavioral covenant, also a structural solution, became the tool for change. It was a public agreement in which participants held themselves and one another to account for their behavior. The bishop knew that in his political role, he could change nothing. His structural response depended on the human relations frame for its success.

The Lesson

In the congregation where my brilliant plan for restructuring collapsed, my neglect of relationships was the culprit. The Baptist pastor who tried to grow his church before addressing their anxiety regrets that he did not begin with relationship building. The bishop above knew that the doorway to reconciliation was not through his power but through relationship. Do we see a pattern here? *The human relations frame is the foundation for any and every task in ministry.* This is because, as each of these examples demonstrate, trust must be established. Without trust, of the leader, of one another, and of God, none of our goals have a chance.

The human relations frame is the essential starting point of effective ministry. As shall be addressed later, this is true even in corporation-size congregations.

Identity

When I arrived at a church in the mid-2000s, their most recent mission statement said the church was "an intentionally inclusive community of believers." During the period in which this was written, the 1990s, this was an LGBTQ-affirming statement. Every Sunday I began to announce that the church was an "intentionally inclusive community of believers." When there was pushback, I pointed to the mission statement.

Soon after I began this practice, I received a visit from the chair of the Christian Education committee, who admitted discomfort with saying that "out loud," but added: "If we're going to say we're intentionally inclusive, why limit it to lesbian and gay folks? How can we be 'intentionally inclusive' of children in worship, for instance?"

That was the beginning of a church-wide transformation. Over time, LGBTQ folks became a regular part of the life and leadership of the church; but intentional inclusion broadened into an attitude of hospitality across the board. Church greeters saw themselves as the front line of intentional inclusion. There was extra effort made to welcome minorities and people of other nationalities. Children and youth became a regular part of worship leadership. Because the words "intentional inclusion" and "open and affirming" were prominent on the website, many people, gay and straight, started attending because they shared those values and wanted their children to learn them in church. Intentional inclusion helped motivate the church to welcome homeless people into their building for a hospitality ministry. When a new mission statement was adopted, it was critical to keep the phrase "intentionally inclusive community of believers." Intentional inclusion had become, per Butler Bass, an intentional practice of the congregation.

For me, a crowning moment came when an adult child of the church, raised hearing that it was "intentionally inclusive" ever since she was a preteen, turned down a job as a coach at a "Christian" school because she would not pledge to report any student with sexual identity issues. "That's not the Christianity I learned in my church," she told them.

At another church, discipleship is focused on caring for creation and stewardship of the natural world. In some larger churches, there are several such foci going on at once. What they all have in common is that a group of people have organized their discipleship around a shared goal. They have taken the "disciplined" part of "discipleship" seriously—they study it, practice it in their own lives and as a congregation, regularly pray about it together, and are constantly challenging themselves, their church and their community to better themselves at it.

Without discipline and intentionality, it is difficult to build a community. With them, there is transformational power for the community and the individuals in it.

Authorship

One characteristic of effective community organizing is ongoing, nonstop leadership training. For many community organizers, leadership development—by which they mean constantly training people to discover and actuate their individual and corporate power—is the task of community organizing. If the goal is shared power, then leadership training is job one.

An essential side effect of this focus on leadership training is deep investment. People who have a hand in making decisions and implementing mission are more likely to give their time, money, and hearts.

This is as true of faith communities as it is of movement politics. In a way, a pastoral leader's calling is to put herself out of a job. We must train congregants to do the ministry of the church or synagogue effectively. They need to feel a sense of *authorship*. Say Bolman and Deal:

> Excellence requires more than pious sermons from top management; it demands commitment and autonomy at all levels of an

enterprise. How do leaders foster such dedication? As we've said before, 'Leading is giving. Leadership is an ethic, a gift of oneself.' Critical for creating and maintaining excellence is the gift of authorship. . . . Trusting people to solve problems generates higher levels of motivation and better solutions. *The leader's responsibility is to create conditions that promote authorship* (italics mine). Individuals need to see their work as meaningful and worthwhile, to feel personally accountable for the consequences of their efforts, and to get feedback that lets them know the results.[19]

Finding lay leaders is possibly the hardest job of ministry. We commonly say that 20 percent of the congregation does 80 percent of the work. Often leaders are overloaded—after all, the best way to get a job done is to give it to a busy person. The burnout rate among congregational lay leadership is high. Not only is this bad for the church, it is also a pastoral failure—we haven't cared for them, which is a big part of being the people of God.

Authorship, an individual's sense that she is empowered to act on her ideas, is surprisingly difficult to foster in a congregation. There are many impediments: groupthink, which causes an individual to sublimate their goals to what is perceived as the consensus; acedia, when one chooses either by inclination or by the level of difficulty to be passive; authoritarianism, the tendency of certain people to take over, rather than to cultivate leadership skills among others; and the logistical challenge of empowering a large number of individuals in a consensual (volunteer) organization. This is further complicated by the fact that congregations are often communities of the wounded, people who have gathered because of their need rather than because they have goals they want to accomplish. This, of course, is why authorship must be promoted: wounded people need to rediscover that they have power to act and to lead.

Often congregational leaders, lay and clergy, are hampered by a failure of imagination. We don't think beyond the 20 percent who do most of the work. If a new member shows some leadership ability, we immediately put them on the congregation's board. We rarely have an "onboarding" process, in which leadership can be cultivated by degrees. Consequently, we risk alienating or burning out enthusiastic volunteers. And finally, our training for board members is often truncated and unimaginative. After all, if it's too complex we're afraid they won't come to the training!

19. Bolman and Deal, *Reframing Organizations*, 415–16. Note that while I tie it into the human relations frame, Bolman and Deal categorize authorship as the "leadership contribution" of the structural frame (415).

Ideally, leadership training starts the day a visitor walks in the door. At the most basic level, it begins with the new member process and the way you familiarize them with the congregation. This is where they are introduced to the history, values, mission, and practices that make the congregation who it is. Shared history and values are the essential baseline for good leadership.

Newer members should not be rushed into leadership roles. Nothing can be more discouraging to a new member than discovering too soon how the sausage is made, or to be forced to do a job for which they are unprepared. At the most basic level, they should be encouraged to volunteer, try their hand at various things as they find what best addresses their spiritual need. As (or if) they show an interest in certain areas, the next phase can be asking them to teach a short course, organize the next sandwich drop-off for the homeless, or to serve on a committee or a team. Let them experience specific, time-limited leadership responsibilities.

There is a difference between committees and teams. Committees generally have broad overarching responsibilities, are part of a governance system with fiduciary responsibilities, and often require a time commitment of a year or longer. Teams, however, are targeted to a specific purpose and have a limited if intense time commitment. Teams allow their members to be creative and imaginative. Teams promote authorship and teach leadership. Others have written extensively on the advantage of the team model in churches.[20]

Teams are an excellent way to engage people with a passion for a particular issue but who are hesitant to commit to the long-term responsibility of serving on a board or committee. Teams can be created to try out new or alternative ideas in the church or to implement one-time events such as fellowship meals, retreats, or a special worship service. Congregational leaders can be intentional in assigning new or less active members to these specific tasks. As church consultant and author John Wimberly points out, most millennials and Gen-Zers "don't even know what a committee is. They have functioned in teams since grade school and continued to do so in school, work, and so on."[21] In his own ministry, Wimberly's church ultimately eliminated committees and did all their work by teams, to good effect.

20. E.g., Wimberly, *Mobilizing Congregations*.

21. Wimberly, personal conversation and notes.

Leader Training

The pastor or rabbi must be intentional about putting the right leaders in the right places and analyzing the effectiveness of the institution's structure. This means engagement in who gets elected to serve in which office, who chairs which committee—for that matter who is on which committee—and very importantly, how they are trained. What do officers of the church need to know to do their job? That is a vital question the cleric needs to answer. If we're simply taking a day to familiarize them with the Book of Order (or whatever your denomination requires for leader training) we are almost certainly teaching them nothing that empowers them to be leaders.

The most important characteristic to instill in church leaders today is adaptivity. "Adaptive leadership," writes Heifetz, "is specifically about change that enables the capacity to thrive."[22] The FCT reports that vital and healthy congregations are "innovative and open to change."[23] It presents a stark perspective on the decline of congregations and the necessity of adaptability. "The research is clear that this moment demands real change if a large percentage of faith communities are to survive the next twenty years with spiritual vibrancy and ministry effectiveness."[24]

Faith communities are notoriously bad at adaptation. In large part this is because lay leaders and clergy view their roles as *stewards* rather than as *leaders*. They believe their main responsibility is to maintain the homeostasis and are fearful to try new things.

The Faith Communities Today report observes:

> Religious leaders must be willing to champion innovative visions and novel ways forward just as they did over the past eighteen months (of the pandemic). These adaptive leaders will have to sustain this energy and passion to communicate the necessity for change, strategize a path forward, rally congregational will, and then mediate conflictual moments that will inevitably arise. Dynamic change also requires a body of individuals willing to embrace new paths.[25]

---

22. Heifetz et al., *Practice of Adaptive Leadership*, 14.

23. Thumma, "Twenty Years of Congregational Change," 27.

24. Thumma, "Twenty Years of Congregational Change," 29.

25. Thumma, "Twenty Years of Congregational Change," 20.

Creating adaptive leadership can be a slow, cumulative process. There are certain key elements to developing adaptive leadership that need to be incorporated into leadership training.

Leaders need to know the congregation's history—but not simply as a list of facts; rather they should understand its emotional history. Help them observe repeating patterns good and bad, past behavior in times of crisis or success, ways in which the history illustrates the values that are still held dear and ways in which the congregation may have failed to live up to them or changed them due to changing times; and ways that it has handled adaptive challenges in the past.

Officer training must put a premium on the core values of the congregation. Shared values and history must be the common ground of your leadership team. Often leader training is so focused on structural matters that core values are neglected or presumed. Understanding core values is a much more important leadership quality than structural knowledge. It is critical for adaptive leaders because in times of change it helps them discern what is important and what is not.

Core values are not only values particular to your congregation, but the overarching values of the faith tradition. For instance, at a church where radical hospitality is practiced, the officer training might ground that hospitality theologically in God's grace. In my officer training, I spend more time on the PCUSA Book of Confessions, a compendium of our theological statements over centuries, than I do on our denominational rulebook. If they need to know something in the rulebook, they can look it up; but the deepest values of our faith should be ingrained.

Of course, leaders need to understand structural matters—not only denominational polity, but the congregation's manual of operations, its budget, its attendance and giving numbers. All this needs to be contextualized in the larger dynamics of community, denomination, and nation. If attendance numbers are in decline, it's important to know that attendance is in decline nationally and how your decline compares to national trends.

Especially in the aftermath of the pandemic, leaders need to develop a culture of experimentation. This is especially challenging unless it is consistently and persistently emphasized. This is one reason leadership training needs to begin the minute people walk in the door. Unless authorship has been instilled and emphasized consistently in other aspects of congregational life it will be hard to instill it in the officers of the church. Dealing with pandemic restrictions and limitations forced many congregations to make radical changes to maintain their ministry. That has laid groundwork for ongoing experimental, creative thinking.

It is vital that congregations intentionally practice diversity in leader recruitment and training. They must induct new people into existing committees and structures, or stagnation will develop. One way to do that is to invite targeted individuals who seem to have leadership potential to attend your officer training classes. There's no need to wait until they have the job title.[26]

A final point to consider in this age of low attendance, closing congregations, and fewer clergy is that lay leaders need to understand themselves taking on roles that in the past have been assigned to clergy. There are three dangers here. One is that this is a daunting task and not many lay people will feel up to the challenge. Another is that there are always power-hungry individuals who are only too glad to take on the anxious power this role implies.

And the third is that many congregations, judicatories, and denominations simply are not structured for this. Clergy are not trained for it. This lay training will often land in the lap of judicatories who want to focus on ground level leadership development. There is already some movement, and success, in this direction.

"Leadership is an ethic, a gift of oneself," Bolman and Deal remind us.[27] Some people have natural leadership ability, but anyone can learn it. *Servant leadership* is a balancing act between confidence in one's abilities and opinions—one's power—and the humble desire to submit your power to the congregation's mission and community.

Leadership requires cultivation. Pastors and rabbis should prioritize the education and pastoral care of lay leaders. In most faith traditions leadership is characterized as a calling, a spiritual discipline. Faith leaders should meet regularly with lay leaders to mentor them and to support them in the challenges that attend their lives. Congregational leadership both affects and is affected by a leader's personal life. Providing pastoral care and mentoring to lay leaders (and employees!) must be a top priority of anyone in a management position in a faith community. In program and corporation sized churches, it is wise for the senior pastor personally to provide pastoral care to the lay leadership.

Denominations need to focus on developing leadership skills in their clergy. *This must start in seminary.* Sadly, leadership skills are rarely in the curriculum. "The strangest thing they didn't teach me in seminary," said

---

26. Heifetz et al., *Practice of Adaptive Leadership*, 14–17.

27. Bolman and Deal, *Reframing Organizations*, 415–16.

one recent graduate, "is how to do church." This is a deeply disturbing failure since "leadership is itself a therapeutic modality . . . that differentiates the clergy as family counselors from all other members of the helping professions."[28] I further argue that *leadership peculiarly defines a cleric's role and makes it dramatically different from any other civilian profession.* Few other professionals enter their very first job as an organization's leader!

Many judicatories take training their clergy seriously. It is essential that leadership training is lifelong; but to fail to offer it in seminary sends many clergy to congregations either as sheep to the slaughter or foxes to guard the henhouse.

Seminaries and judicatories also need to develop ways to screen potential faith leaders for leadership qualities, especially self-differentiation and people skills. Some people who graduate our seminaries don't have them and never will. The damage they can do to vulnerable congregations in this challenging moment is incalculable.

Treating all our members as potential leaders whose ideas and contributions are appreciated and valued is essential to creating an atmosphere of community, celebration, and faithful discipleship. Without it, our congregations are hospitals for sick souls. With it, our congregations will thrive as outposts of God's Beloved Community.

Power in the Political Frame

The political frame considers organizations from the perspective of power struggle between different interests for scarce resources and competing goals. Negotiation takes center stage.[29] This is often viewed as the most unpleasant way to look at congregational dynamics. How many of us have heard (or said) "I hate politics in the church!" But if humans are involved, politics is inevitable. Jesus says, "Where two or three are gathered in my name, I am there in the midst of them" (Matt 18:20). As it happens, one colloquial definition of politics is "two or more people together." To be a community of faith *is* to be political.

Earlier I told the story of the council that censured a well-off deacon for bullying and undermining behavior. This incident had not only structural (rules-based) and human relations (pastoral care) implications, but political ones. Censuring an officer has political implications that might

28. Friedman, *Generation to Generation*, 2.

29. Bolman and Deal, *Reframing Organizations*, 191.

have put off some church councils from acting. The public censure was a major blow to the long-term, unhealthy (as opposed to healthy) "unofficial" power brokers.

But there were casualties. Not only did the offender, his wife and his mother leave the church, but one of the women whom he had bullied stopped attending. The person who'd secretly recorded the nominating proceedings never returned to church.

When politics raises its head, there are always casualties. It is always a matter of shame that people get hurt in a congregation. It is also inevitable. Most of us go into ministry to help people, not hurt them. This creates a clash between the human relations and political frames. It's why many of us are offended by "politics" in church or synagogue. The problem is that you can't have humans without having politics.

Reframing Politics

Religious people resist politics because its hard-headed focus on power dynamics seems to clash with the ideal community we want to promote and be. We see a conflict between the political and the symbolic frames. But the political frame serves up a necessary dose of realism. Politics—the clash between interests; tensions around resources, purpose, meaning; who is included and who is excluded; the ways people mobilize to attain goals and to build a base of support; and all the emotional impact that has on the system—is the sea in which humans swim and the way forward toward our goals. It can help us clarify and unify around purpose, but it also sheds uncomfortable light on all the ways we still fall short of perfection. It gives us a strategic mindset and challenges us to get real in our ongoing pursuit of the ideal rather than imagining we have already arrived or that the path will be easy.

Religious people sometimes assume that politics is about attaining self-serving power at the cost of other people's interests. Politics is viewed as selfish. Religious people aspire to selflessness.

That it can be used selfishly doesn't mean it has to be. Community organizers emphasize *enlightened self-interest.* Enlightened self-interest means that, broadly speaking, what's good for all is good for one; and what's good for one, is good for all. Obviously, that can't always be the case. Religious people often mistake enlightened self-interest for self-centeredness. That's not how community organizers think of it. Self-interest is what someone cares about—their passion.

When I was first involved with faith-based community organizing, I went with our organizer and a team of leaders to meet with the vice superintendent of alternative education for the public schools. He was initially wary of us. Our organizer, Mark, started to ask him what got him interested in working on alternative education. The administrator told us about his early work at a Native American school. There he became committed to the need to vary educational approaches to give everyone the opportunities that education offers. Mark shared how his work as an Americorps volunteer had affected him in a similar way. All of us shared that we held the same belief about education. The administrator was enthusiastic and warm by the time the meeting ended. Discovering this shared passion—our mutual self-interest—made conversation, planning, and teamwork with the administrator much easier in the future, facilitating important initiatives.

Organizers combine the human relations and political frames brilliantly through relational meetings. These are purposeful individualized meetings that are two-way conversations about passions, interests, hopes and dreams. Clergy who engage in relational meetings with leaders and potential leaders in their congregations experience better mutual understanding and cooperation and more differentiated leadership.

It is certainly true that in politics (and life) self-interest can be selfish. But to frame self-interest as entirely selfish misunderstands it. In most honest political discourse, people want what they want not only for themselves but for others. They are not driven by selfishness or self-centeredness but passion for something larger than themselves. To frame self-interest as selfish and therefore immoral contributes to the demonization of differentiation. Often potential leaders are told, or tell themselves, the things they feel strongest about are selfish. Opportunities are quashed even before they are expressed.

Resources

Earlier we discussed the PCUSA's split after the vote to allow ordination of LGBTQ individuals. The churches that left were some of the most resource-rich congregations in the PCUSA. Resources—financial, programmatic, or human—are often not fully appreciated in faith communities. *Resources create power.* A minority with good resources inevitably has a great deal of power in any structure. Alienating them has consequences. The distribution of resources is a key concern of the political frame and a real test of how to balance self-interest with the common good.

It is important to remember that the goal of your politics is *shared power.* To allow the hoarding of resources by a few undermines that goal. At the same time, we must recognize that those who are hoarding the resources are certain that they, too, are acting for the common good—and they may have a good argument! *To use the political frame to resolve the inevitable tensions caused when building shared power is an act of mutual respect.* It acknowledges that both sides have truth and power they are bringing to the table. To negotiate means that both sides are willing to consider a competing view of the common good.

When a programmed-size church hired a new, young, talented, and energetic music director, he immediately wanted to launch a campaign to raise money for long-overdue updates and improvements on the organ. The organ work he envisioned would cost well over half a million dollars.

To have a large campaign for the organ alone would cause huge controversy in the church. Fifteen years before, the church had been mainly centered around music, but Christian education, justice, and diversity had suffered. Lay leaders and staff had worked hard to change that direction and succeeded. Recently goals had been set to improve disability access and provide resources for the mission and youth programs, but these had been stalled by limited funding. To have an organ campaign when other needs were not met would cause division and resentment.

It was decided that a comprehensive capital campaign would address all the issues. This allowed the church to use the power of people's appreciation of one set of resources to shore up the power of people's support for others. It used self-interest to the advantage of everyone. The church probably couldn't build up momentum to raise capital for the non-organ-related goals they had set, despite broad agreement they were critical. On the other hand, they could easily drum up financial support from a handful of generous music lovers (including many nonmembers) for the organ project. Combining the two brought the good will of those who wanted to attain the mission and building goals while bringing the financial resources of those who supported the music program.

One challenge was that the organ project's costs were more than those of all the other projects combined. Ultimately, as costs skyrocketed, every item in the campaign had to take a cut. Because of its size, the organ project took the biggest cut of all. This helped address a question so many had asked—Why should they spend so much on the organ?—with the answer that there was much more included in the campaign; and every project, including the organ, had to take a cut.

Everyone who brought a campaign project was a strong advocate. That's how it should be. Negotiating is hard, especially in a congregational setting. We avoid it because we mistake it for division. But it needs to happen more often. It happens best when people are ardent for their causes but, once they've made their case, they recognize the need for compromise for the good of the whole.

The Political Frame and Pastoral Anxiety

When I was a young pastor, my anxiety over how people feel and whether they liked me kept me constantly reactive. I was caught between my own self-focus and the human relations frame, with no real way to escape the confusing emotional whirlpool this tension created in my work and in my life.

Community organizing introduced me to an entirely new way of thinking. I could think strategically about the challenges I faced. This enabled me to transcend the emotions and anxieties that controlled my actions and instead step onto what Ron Heifetz calls "the balcony,"[30] able not merely to see the big picture but also to develop thoughtful approaches to address emotionally charged issues and redirect them to the larger good, for myself, others, and the reign of God.

The political frame enabled me to control my own anxiety and to reframe emotion-charged situations—and all situations are emotion-charged!—for my family, friends, and parishioners. *The political frame is a powerful resource to transcend emotional dysfunction and manage personal and systemic anxiety.*

Power Analysis

A couple of years prior to the PCUSA's decision to welcome LGBTQ people into ordained leadership, my Texas church, known for its welcome of gay individuals and families, hosted a former PCUSA moderator to speak on a book he'd published recently on how he, as a former Evangelical, had come to believe that LGBTQ inclusion was essential to the gospel. I looked upon

30. Heifetz et al., *Practice of Adaptive Leadership*, 33.

this entirely from the perspective of having a prominent PCUSA leader and scholar speak at the church without considering the symbolic implications of the topic.

There was immediate, and to me surprising, backlash. It was from a group of members who were uncomfortable with the church's increasing inclusivity. The group's leader was a young man who had recently joined and had almost immediately been elected to the board. I doubt he realized how many lesbian and gay folk were in the congregation. Had I misread how "open and affirming" the congregation really was?

Tensions rose throughout the congregation. Lesbian and gay members who had viewed the church as a safe harbor were outraged and frightened. Middle-of-the-road members worried we were going too far, too fast. The staff determined the best response was to invite an "opposing" speaker to speak the week after our original speaker.

I used a tool I'd learned from community organizing called a *power analysis*. It analyzes what relationships are at work in any organizational system to engage those dynamics to effect a positive result. I developed a power analysis and gave it to each staff member and a few choice church leaders. Questions included:

1. If you wanted support for a project, who are the three people you would most be able to count on for moral support?

2. Of those, whose support would be the most effective?

3. Which three people would be most likely to resist any project you advanced?

4. Of those, whose resistance would be most effective?

5. Name the three people you believe have the most influence over opinion *within* the church.

6. Name the three people who have the most influence *beyond* the church. Where do they have that influence, and with whom?

7. Who do you think are the best financial givers? (Up to five.)

8. What official group in the church has the most power?

9. What "unofficial" group in the church has the most power?

10. What do you believe (or know) people outside of the church are saying about us? (One or more.)

11. What would you like outside people to say about our church five years from now? (One or more.)

12. What is the biggest challenge facing the church in the next year?

Based on our analysis of the results, we determined whom to ask for support for our plan, whom we needed to look out for, whom we most needed to reassure so that things wouldn't get further inflamed, and who could be trusted in a time of crisis. We also affirmed our shared commitment to LGBTQ inclusion. We identified a spokesperson: an openly gay man who was not in a relationship and had been a member for decades. Our power analysis had identified him as the most trusted member of the congregation. He immediately agreed to be the face of the speaker series we had developed. His calm style and the affection that people felt for him would prove critical to the positive resolution of this crisis.

The rest of the staff made a point of contacting every name that had popped up on the lists. The list was shorter than you might think since we'd identified many of the same people. We listened to their perspective and told them where we stood and what we hoped to accomplish (an open affirmation that the church welcomes LGBTQ individuals and couples). We told them that despite our preferences, we wanted a free and fair hearing of both sides and would accept the consequences. We were practicing Friedman's rule to "define self and continue to stay in touch."[31]

The two Sunday nights, with a week between them, in which our speakers spoke were tense. But by the end of the process, the congregation had reached an extraordinary level of clarity. They had found themselves intrigued by the former moderator's presentation and repelled by the speaker against LGBTQ inclusion. Those in the middle decided they preferred open inclusion to the "don't ask, don't tell" philosophy they'd held before. The session made clear its position that St. Stephen is "an intentionally inclusive community of believers." Later, when some left the church over the General Assembly's official vote to allow LGBTQ ordination, the vast majority who remained felt that St. Stephen's position had already been clarified and were able to weather the storm.

There were casualties. A few families and individuals left the church because of the debate and as I said, when the denomination clarified its position, we lost even more. But most stayed, with a stronger sense of shared

---

31. Friedman, *Generation to Generation*, 229.

purpose, mission, and community. To this day, one of the most stated reasons people join the church is that it welcomes LGBTQ persons.

Pastors and Politics

A corporation-size church pastor had come to a moral conclusion on a difficult issue and began to lead the church in that direction. Knowing this was a controversial topic, but also trusting the spirit of a congregation he had served for years, he gradually rolled out steps that would allow the church to come to acceptance. Throughout, he was open with his board about his goals. The pushback seemed gentle, and the leaders appeared more open as time passed. Then he was blindsided by a group of the most powerful members of the church, many of them serving officers, who came to him in private and told him they wanted his resignation. They had aligned support from his judicatory executive, who decided that he had been "moving too fast," and it was best he should leave. His wife, who ran the church day school, was informed she was no longer employed. The couple left quickly and landed on their feet in another community. But it left scars. The attack wasn't just political—it was personal.

A community organizer once told me, "Jesus teaches that we should be wise as serpents but gentle as doves; but the truth is that many churches are wise as doves and gentle as serpents!" Any cleric leading change has a target on her back. Especially in larger congregations, where enormous power seethes like magma ready to erupt, much of what keeps the institution healthy depends on how well the leader negotiates competing interests and can build up and exercise political capital. For the pastor, this risks being a zero-sum game. Idealists, including those who share her values, may become impatient with how "risk averse" she is. Others may view her as "moving too fast." Change, especially in religious institutions, is like trying to bring the Titanic about before it hits the iceberg—it can't just turn on a dime! And sadly, the iceberg is more likely to sink the pastor than the congregation.

Every religious leader needs to be adept at politics, but this is especially true in a corporation-size congregation. Its abundant resources, institutional clout, and congregation of community leaders and the wealthy give it extraordinary ability to do good, but also create intense power dynamics that can eat naïve or clumsy pastors and staff alive. They can also be alienating to parishioners seeking spiritual sustenance or discipleship opportunities, who may end up invisible to clergy and staff whose time and energy are consumed by power politics. These dynamics can unintentionally mow down those who don't play the power game.

The Political Implications of Clergy Differentiation

Clergy differentiation, being clear on who you are and where you stand, could be viewed as a relational matter: one is simply establishing clear boundaries and defining oneself. But if one is differentiating with an eye to systemic change, it is a political act with political implications. Ignoring this is naïve and self-destructive. Pastors and rabbis seeking change will deal with angry parishioners who will have little hesitation to be political themselves. A differentiated leader can make her followers more differentiated as well. She can also infuriate and offend undifferentiated congregants. And don't be surprised if it gets personal.

A pastor at one church received hundreds of letters from a handful of parishioners insulting and threatening him and his family. Perhaps because he viewed these letters as a pastoral matter requiring confidentiality rather than a political matter, he did not report them to the church board until too much damage had been done to his personal morale for him to continue at that church. Other pastors have found themselves under the microscope of their regional councils because angry parishioners have complained to their bishop, district superintendent, or executive presbyter. And it is a common practice for parishioners to cut back or withhold giving when they disagree with a pastor or rabbi's leadership.

All these are political acts and need to be treated as such. Jesus himself (or early church leaders building on his teaching) knew these were political acts and set up reasonable guidelines for dealing with them.

> If another member of the church sins against you, go and point out the fault when the two of you are alone. If the member listens to you, you have regained that one. But if you are not listened to, take one or two others along with you so that every word may be confirmed by the evidence of two or three witnesses. If the member refuses to listen to them, tell it to the church; and if the offender refuses to listen even to the church, let such a one be to you as a gentile or a tax collector. (Matt 18:15–17)

Jesus advises us first to treat "sin" as a pastoral, or human relations, matter; but if that fails, you engage others. The matter has become political.

"Sin," of course, doesn't describe every conflict or disagreement in a church. It's not a sin to withhold your pledge or lower it because you question the direction things are going. And there are many reasons to treat these and other conflicts between pastor and parishioner as private rather than public. But there is a difference between something being "private" and something being "confidential."

Confidential means that a pastor, as a professional, must keep this interaction, including every word said and every action taken, as something that must stay between her and her client or parishioner. It assumes that what was said or done would not have happened were it not in the context of the "Cone of Silence" implied by the pastor/parishioner confidential relationship. There are legal implications to confidentiality. In difficult pastoral interactions, one may need to consult another practitioner of confidentiality—a therapist, the executive of your judicatory, a lawyer or doctor—on how to handle a delicate matter. You may need to report it to the authorities.

Private interactions, in contrast, are not confidential. Each party involved can decide for themselves whether to tell someone else about what happened. In private interactions secrets are not divulged. To say something is private is another way of saying it's not public—*yet.*

It is important for pastors to understand that if the interaction is about *you* particularly then many of the normal guidelines for confidential conversation don't apply. If you are threatened or accused of something you did not do, if you are intimidated or bullied, if your family is threatened, then all bets are off. And these things happen to pastors and rabbis. A sexual come-on by a parishioner is harassment, which in most congregations and judicatories is addressed in a harassment policy—if it's reported.

It is not uncommon for the lines between confidential and private conversations and actions to become skewed in the congregation, or for parishioners to knowingly take advantage of those gray areas.

Pastors and rabbis are taught to understand and respect the power of their roles in congregations and to be alert to the temptation to abuse that power. But we must not make the mistake of believing that all the power in that relationship goes one way. Our parishioners are generally capable adults. They have power, too. Respect it. Protect them, but protect yourself, too.

Reclaiming Power in Congregational and Community Ministry

Politics beyond the Congregation

Congregations *must* be political. As Bonhoeffer says, the church is only the church when it is there for others. Congregations make a mistake when they believe that whatever challenges they face are only internal. The crisis facing religion in America today is the result of our lack of engagement for the common good. Partisan Christians are not working for the public good but for their own interests. Even congregations that are not over-political are often perceived as self-involved, making little contribution to the communities where they live. In contrast, congregations doing well today "are active in the local community"[32] and perceived to be making a positive civic contribution.

Religious people misunderstand what "political" means. Often, they think it means "controversial." When they ask the rabbi not to be political, they really mean "don't stir the pot." Other times they identify certain matters of which the pastor speaks, or on which the church acts, as political because to the accuser these issues seem (and maybe are) partisan. Properly, to be "political" means engaged for the public good. What that might be is often a matter of controversy!

Some think any "politics" is bad because they imagine that separation of church and state means that congregations should stay out of local, regional, or national politics. They misunderstand their role in a democracy. "Separation of church and state" means that no religion should dominate or have the final say in a democratic community. But religious organizations have every right to be one of the voices at the public table, engaging on matters where they share values with other interest groups working for the larger good of the community. Democracy means we have no right to dominate but every right, even an obligation, to participate—the same as every citizen or group.

One question that consultants ask congregations in crisis is "Who would miss you if you were gone?" This gets to the heart of the problem. Congregations, like individuals, operate in Dr. King's "web of mutuality." One way to understand "love your neighbor as yourself" is that *we have no self without our neighbor.* Our relationships define and shape us. This is as true of congregations as it is of individuals. No church is an island, entire to itself. Yet often they act that way.

32. Thumma, "Twenty Years of Congregational Change," 27.

Congregations sometimes get involved in politics by taking a stand on a particular issue. While this act of differentiation can be a good start, the real heart of political engagement is relationships. Congregations should be busy building relationships long before they feel moved to take a public stand. The most effective faith-engaged work happens in local communities, where congregations work together with one another and agencies, local government, and nonprofits on matters such as homelessness, addiction, affordable housing, and racial justice. These are larger matters of public good where alliances build shared power and public trust. A small congregation can make a big difference by building good relationships with diverse partners toward shared goals. And there is a payoff to the congregation in good will, public recognition, and self-esteem.

Public Leadership, Risk, and Power

It is not uncommon for clergy to take personal stands on matters of public importance, say, participating in a protest, while wearing a collar or otherwise indicating their professional standing. This can be a good symbolic act of differentiation. But wearing the collar implies representing your congregation. Be prepared for a backlash.

But also, be prepared that *it may not make much difference.* Congregants might dislike it but say nothing; or pat you on the back but do nothing. You can make the case that you're showing community leadership, but if you think you are leading the congregation, you are wrong. It is not leadership to take a position. Actions should produce reactions. *To lead, not only must you differentiate, you must also agitate.* Real leadership will create pushback. If you aren't getting it, stir the pot. "What do you think of what I did? If that's what you think, what do you want to do about it?" A leader must intentionally use an act of differentiation to move her constituency forward. Otherwise, the action has no power and builds no power.

This is also true in the public square. It is not uncommon for a cleric, because of how outspoken he is, to become the identified face of a cause, the first person to get interviewed on the news or called upon by civic leaders—and at the same time *have no following.* Power brokers love this. It gives the impression (a) that they are doing something by talking to you and (b) that you are a lone voice crying in the wilderness—really no one else feels the way you do. You have no real power and have built no power.

Clergy can ally with one another toward shared goals that their congregations are unready or unwilling to address. Ecumenical cooperation is a powerful public act of shared power. But again, do not imagine this doesn't impact your congregation. Even if you don't intend it, your actions will produce a reaction. Your public leadership will agitate some in your congregation either to dissent or support.

Nothing you do as clergy happens vacuum-sealed from your congregation. If you were hoping they wouldn't notice, you are not being honest, or a leader. To put it plainly, you are not leading if you are not organizing people or money. Symbolic acts are powerful only insofar as they organize people or money.

There is no such thing as accidental leadership. When one acts in the clergy role, be intentional and strategic about what you hope to accomplish, in community, congregation, or both.

You Could Lose—But You Could Win

And be aware of the risk. Any battle worth winning is worth losing. Don't expect universal gratitude when taking a public stand. Anticipate pushback. Be aware you could lose. Make sure it's worth it.

The awareness that you could lose gives you great strategic insight. The more aware you are that you could lose, the more likely you are to identify and shore up your weaknesses. And the more likely you are to lose on one front but win on another.

When Fort Worth housing advocates determined to stand against the T's decision to replace day-passes with two-hour passes, they went to clergy, and they in turn went to their congregations. The real power to bring about change would not come from anti-poverty activists, nonprofits, or clergy but from regular people. Congregants from different institutions met with one another, learned, and strategized together, protested, and met with public figures. Dozens of people turned out at the T's board and city council meetings. Relationships developed. We lost that battle but strengthened support for the unhoused across the community.

Within my church, more people became committed to the unhoused than ever. Political leaders became aware of unhappy constituents and the challenge of congregations organizing together. Homelessness has become the key unifying issue for the religious community, with direct benefits to the unhoused and agencies working with them.

With good planning and a strong base, "losing" becomes a relative term. A loss becomes a tool for education. The base you've built can be directed to new opportunities. Often you have lighted passions that continue to burn. You have also built a reputation in the community for standing for something and built relationships that open doors. All this strengthens you for the next challenge.

This is important for congregations to know. One of the main reasons congregations do not act (on many things!) is *risk*. Risk of failure; risk of alienating people or losing money; risk of public embarrassment. But any battle worth winning is worth losing. Congregations often miss opportunities because they are risk averse. *Perhaps the biggest adaptive change necessary in congregations is to accept the necessity of risk and to celebrate risk-taking as an act of faith.*

Clergy and Risk

Risk is also the biggest adaptive change facing clergy. Clergy tend toward one or both of two extremes: either they are passionate advocates or over-cautious "peacemongers." Passionate advocates want action now and are impatient with the slow process of bringing a congregation along. They may be poor at motivating people; their passion can be inspiring but also off-putting. Their impatience manifests as unwillingness to take the risk of developing a following. They become lone rangers. That isn't leadership. Congregants may admire and respect their pastor or rabbi, but they don't follow her. And clergy need to watch out, because while the congregants may not openly push back, any little slip on the cleric's part can lead them to decide she needs to go. "She's making a bit of a scene in public," they might say, "AND the Smith funeral was too long. It's probably best if she moves on."

Peacemongers, Friedman says, are anxious, feel-good consensus builders, unable to take or defend a stand.[33] They are the opposite of well-differentiated leaders. Risk aversion becomes a moral priority for peacemongers, to whom any tension or unhappiness is the greatest sin and a sign of personal failure. Many clergy are naturally oriented that way.

My natural orientation toward being a peacemonger started in my family of origin, where I played (ineffectively) the role of peacemaker as much to calm my frayed nerves as actually to "fix" my family. Many clergy

---

33. Friedman, *Failure of Nerve*, 15.

are inclined to "fix" things. As a "fixer," I imagined my role to be neutral. Self-differentiation was anathema because it undermined that imagined role. Training in systems theory, good supervision, experience in community organizing and the school of hard knocks beat much of it out of me, but I remain vigilant for signs of it. I believe in peacemaking and can be a good mediator, but the line between peacemaker and peacemonger is razor thin.

Dysfunctional systems love peacemongers. Peacemongers imagine themselves as healers and work hard to understand every perspective and smooth over every problem. I played this role when I was a young chaplain at a halfway house. I tried to mediate tensions between the social workers and their boss, tensions that the clients used to play them against one another. I patted myself on the back for how willing everyone was to open up to me, even my bosses. I now understand that they were happy for my mediation because it gave the impression that they were all working hard for resolution when they really weren't. I became essential to the homeostasis.

Moral leadership is political. It requires balancing passion and patience, clear self-differentiation, and the willingness to negotiate and compromise. Most of all, it requires risk. *There can be no moral leadership and no substantive change without being political.* Whether within a congregation or beyond it, allies must be found, coalitions built, resources allocated, and resistance reckoned with. Power must be accumulated to accomplish your goal. Any attempt to be moral without being political is toothless.

This is as true for congregations as it is for clergy. A congregation's willingness to risk a distinctive, differentiated position can enhance its standing in the community and attract people for whom that issue matters. It can energize and focus its members. It can make it a leader in their community. This focus can be especially helpful to shepherding- and programmed-size congregations. Churches can build their discipleship around it. This identity keeps smaller congregations vital and vibrant. Congregations that take distinctive stands on homelessness, immigrant ministries, creation care, and so on, benefit inside, in the church, and outside, in the community.

However, settling on one position is not always easy and requires politicking within the congregation. And even when you settle on it, not everyone will care for it. But politicking well done, balancing clarity with a willingness to listen—differentiating but staying in touch—will leave the dissenters with enough peace that they can appreciate other aspects of the church's ministry without feeling alienated by what they disagree with. It will help that the position taken is not merely the cleric's, but that of a lot of their friends in the congregation as well.

The Challenge of Ecumenical Moral Leadership

During the pandemic, two Black Fort Worth pastors reached out to a largely white clergy group and asked for a meeting. They wanted to build an inter-religious coalition to promote racial unity as the community prepared for the trial of the former police officer who had killed a young Black woman, Atatiana Jefferson, in her home a few years before.

The clergy group was a coalition of mainline and Jewish congregations with four decades of history. In the past, a Black pastor or two had been part of it, as had a few Hispanics. The group was a respected force in Fort Worth, but it was largely white. White and non-white clergy and congregations essentially operated in separate spheres, as did evangelical and non-evangelical groups. The two Black pastors who called the meeting were taking the risk of breaking that barrier.

The challenges the new group had to overcome are illustrative of the difficulties of building interfaith coalitions. White mainline clergy were "liberal" and many of them were women, gay, or both. Black clergy were largely conservative and evangelical; interacting with women, LGBTQ, and non-Christian clergy was new for them. The dominance of Christian clergy made things awkward for rabbis and was off-putting for Unity, Buddhist, and Muslim leaders.

Our goal was racial unity. We could set aside other differences in pursuit of that goal. Our diversity was a key source of our power. But setting aside such differences is easier said than done. To build unity in Fort Worth, we first had to build it within our coalition. This involved challenging conversations to address cultural differences between the races, religions, and economic statuses we represented. These conversations sometimes felt like they were hijacking the mission. Yet these differences were the reason we had not worked together in the past. They had to be addressed. What held things together was an overarching atmosphere of good will, a willingness to learn, and a commitment to our larger purpose.

For such a coalition to work requires a value that every religion celebrates but often forgets to practice: humility. To work toward racial unity, dialogue about differences was necessary, but in the final analysis, everyone needed to put aside their pet "trigger" issue to work toward the larger goal.

How well they would be able to do that would determine what form their mission would take and how successful it would be.

Ecumenical cooperation is an essential antidote to the decreasing relevance of the faith community's voice in public discourse. It is how we prove that a diverse, multi-religious and cross-cultural community is possible and a benefit to civic discourse, as opposed to the Christian dominionist message or the distrust of faith institutions in the larger culture.

But too often we assume that coalitions that represent only a fraction of the faith community are adequate to the task. We don't want to take the risk of having real conversations with people whose beliefs or life experience differ from ours.

If shared power is our goal, it must also be our means. If we aren't talking to others, then we aren't respecting them, which means that power won't be shared. Hard conversations lay the groundwork for equal footing and build community.

But to have those conversations, people of faith need to set aside their fears, prejudices, and pride just as much as nonbelievers do. We need to stop pretending like we want to do it and do it.

Individual congregations play an important part in this. Increasingly, congregations are partnering with one another across racial, religious, and cultural boundaries, for prayer meetings, book studies, fellowship, or action. They build bonds of community and respect, as well as one-on-one relationships. This congregation-based work is an essential foundation for larger ecumenical ventures.

The diversity of ecumenical, cross-cultural coalitions gives them power which makes civic leaders take them seriously. But they have more power still if it's not merely the clergy, but the congregants who have aligned toward a shared moral goal. You will never get two congregations to agree on everything. But if they agree on one thing, civic leaders, corporate executives, and elected officials do well to sit up and take notice.

Power in the Symbolic Frame

The Symbolic Frame is the arena of meaning. Meaning is the most important aspect of human existence. "Those who have a 'why' to live can bear almost any 'how,'"[34] psychiatrist Victor Frankl quotes from Nietzsche in

---

34. Frankl, *Man's Search for Meaning,* 76.

Man's Search for Meaning. Frankl speaks of "the self-transcendence of human existence," which he describes as

> the fact that being human always points, and is directed, to something or someone, other than himself—be it a meaning to fulfill or another human being to encounter. The more one forgets himself—by giving himself to a cause to serve or another person to love—the more human he is and the more he actualizes himself. What is called self-actualization is not an attainable aim at all, for the simple reason that the more one would strive for it, the more he would miss it. In other words, self-actualization is possible only as a side-effect of self-transcendence.[35]

Self-transcendence—meaning—is the purpose of religion. Religion infuses the individual, the community and the cosmos with higher purpose that helps us understand who we are and our relationship to all that is.

We use words and images—symbols—to frame this cosmic purposiveness in ways our limited understanding can manage. Symbols point toward those higher things which are beyond our grasp. They are magnificent exercises in imagination that make us better able to grasp mystery.

Religion is the realm of the symbolic. But religion hardly has a corner on the symbol market. Symbols dominate every aspect of human reality. The Golden Arches don't infuse us with higher purpose, but we know what they mean!

Every business has a mission statement. It gives the business a larger purpose that inspires and directs both customers and employees. It makes employees at least somewhat happier to work there and helps them understand what they are supposed to do. It tells customers what they should expect and gives them a reason to give them their business. It reminds employers that the business has a mission and that if it loses sight of that mission, the business will founder and die. Mission statements are commonplace today, an acknowledgement that if a business doesn't recognize the symbolic frame it could fail.

The symbolic is possibly the most powerful frame because it infuses everything else. But it is also the most complicated and elusive of the four frames. No minimum-wage worker works at a fast-food restaurant because she believes in its mission. She works there because she has rent to pay and mouths to feed. Money or family or survival, powerful symbolic values, drive her need for a job, and will likewise drive her satisfaction or

---

35. Frankl, *Man's Search for Meaning*, 110–11.

frustration with the job. To appreciate the power of the symbolic frame, we must understand how complex and varied are the number of symbols that have influence over our lives.

The tension over inviting the pro-LGBTQ speaker to my Fort Worth church was steeped in symbolic importance. To list just a few conflicting symbolic matters at issue:

1. Would the church violate "old" standards of morality, associated with traditional faith, or would it adopt new standards that also represent a new direction?

2. Is the church going to die? If so, what will kill it—breaking from old standards or refusing to adapt?

3. Is the Bible as a symbolic standard open to interpretation, or is it fixed and intractable?

4. Can LGBTQ individuals live with the symbolic "second-class citizen" status of being allowed at the church, but not welcome to be open or to serve in leadership?

5. Do we want to take the risk of acting (either positively or negatively), and in the process take responsibility for whatever comes next; or simply "let things be," and let history take its course? (It's always easier to say "It was God's will" when you never take challenging actions or make hard decisions!)

6. Is Christian faith about judgment or about love?

Issues of life and death, old and new, the nature of God and the universe, interpreting traditions and blazing new paths, adopting or asserting identity, us versus them, fear versus hope, acting or waiting: these are matters of meaning and so are matters of the symbolic frame. Getting this complex frame wrong can undermine everything one hopes to accomplish.

The symbolic frame is always there. If we don't understand what our actions mean to ourselves or others, then nothing else we do will matter.

The challenge is to read other people's minds. How do we know which symbols are driving their behaviors? Fortunately, all our words and actions are fraught with that inner meaning, if only someone knows what to look for—and is looking for it.

Looking at the above case, two symbolic issues seem to have won the day. Both had to do with the nature of Christian community.

A telling moment came when Kit, a highly respected ninety-year-old ruling elder and retired Air Force colonel, very familiar with the Bible and noted for his integrity, stood and challenged the anti-LGBTQ speaker. "Jesus and Paul challenged legalism and told us that love should be our guideline," he said. "But you use the Bible as a legalistic tool to beat people over the head. You, sir, are a legalist. To me, this is not what Christianity is about. I reject your position."

That moment encapsulated the answer to a question: Is God, and therefore Christian community, judgmental—or is God, and therefore Christian community, loving? Kit's answer was that God is love, and that was the answer the church adopted.

A more basic symbolic question was about the role of propriety versus truth-telling. An unspoken value of most mainline churches is that many personal things are best left unsaid because they are uncomfortable to discuss in the open. Sexuality is high on that list. Many of the church's straight members could accept gay individuals, couples, and families in the church if the matter remained somewhat unspoken.

But the anti-inclusion speaker's open and vituperative disdain for LGBTQ people flaunted any acceptable standard of propriety, making all aware of the power of language—and therefore the power of welcoming language.

The symbolic significance of gay couples who sat frowning in the front row with their arms crossed made clear that the speaker's attack was not on an abstract, amorphous other, but on people we knew and loved who were angry and afraid. At a deep level, people realized that if attacks like his happen in the church, issues of gender and sexuality could not be hidden under a bushel. Not to speak out was to participate in violence against our friends. This opened the door for the church's now-open assertion that they welcome LGBTQ people.

No doubt they will need to return to this conversation from time to time in the future, but fifteen years later it's hard to imagine straying too far from the baseline established in these events. People changed internally, in the sense of how they think about the issue and their reasons for attending the church; and externally, in the sense of who now attends.

The Larger Symbols of Our Faith

Christians put the cross and resurrection of Jesus and matters of sin, grace, and redemption front and center of their faith. Jews put the sovereignty of God, their distinct calling to be God's people, and the interpretation of Torah at the symbolic center of their tradition. All religions hope that their symbolic frame is, or is becoming, the driving purpose of the lives of their believers.

But the reality is that these symbols compete in a world full of symbols that pull us different directions, obscuring the faith message or getting enmeshed with it. American Christians can easily confuse patriotism and capitalism with Jesus's message. Likewise, individuals have their own ideas of what it means to be religious, shaped by their own experiences, mentors, and beliefs. Statistically, mainline pastors and rabbis tend to be more liberal than their congregations, but liberalism isn't the same as Christianity or Judaism any more than conservatism is. This is just one more symbolic frame that can illuminate or obscure the true message of our faith.

The Talmud teaches that "It is incumbent upon us neither to attain the Kingdom nor to desist from pursuing it." Symbolically, our faith is a journey that we are on with God and one another. To understand this reminds us that we cannot rest on our laurels, assuming we've already arrived; nor need we give up on ourselves when we feel we've failed.

It also helps us to accept change. Change is the work of congregational leaders. Our scriptures refer to seeds and growth, the changing of seasons, childhood and maturity, conversion, death, and rebirth. The concept of redemption itself is the concept of change. *Metanoia*, the Greek word often translated repent, means "turn around"—change.

But change is a source of tension and fear for many congregations—for that matter, for most people. Change, however, is one of our greatest needs.

Still, that change must be grounded in a symbolic world that is stable, consistent, and overarching, shared, timeless, and unchanging—our faith.

Faith leaders must connect the deepest symbolic meaning of our faith tradition to the lived reality of the congregations and communities that we serve. To the extent we can do this we are strengthening the faith of our congregants and facilitating their ownership of the changes they pursue. When we can connect the work of the church to shared symbolic meaning, then we are attaining shared power.

Do not be surprised if the symbolic frame of a congregation changes over time, or if past symbolic battles need to be re-fought. The symbolic world is as much shaped by changing dynamics as it shapes them. A symbolic battle can be scary, but it is always important. Clergy and congregations who avoid them are avoiding change and growth in the most fundamental frame of human reality.

The Power of the Inter-Subjective

Evolutionary historian Noah Yuval Harrari identifies our ability to create "imagined reality," "something that everyone believes in," as what distinguishes us from other animals. These imagined realities include everything from nations and gods to corporations and money. These things exist because people believe they exist. "As long as this communal belief persists, this imagined reality exerts force in the world."[36] The symbolic world has power both *to* unite and *because* it unites. It enables humans "to change their behavior quickly, transmitting new behaviors to future generations without any need of genetic or environmental change."[37] Harrari calls such communal fictions inter-subjective reality. "Many of history's most important drivers are inter-subjective: law, money, gods, nations."[38]

"Large numbers of strangers can cooperate successfully by believing common myths," Harrari observes.[39] Our symbolic, inter-subjective reality is the real key to shared power. *Since we are defining power as the ability to organize people and resources, then the symbolic is by far the most powerful of the four frames.*

Our faith, which is at least nominally the reason our congregations exist, is one such inter-subjective reality, a reality shared by millions now living and by millions more who have preceded us. But as I mentioned earlier, we live in a world where many inter-subjective realities coexist and can be either cooperative or competitive.

O Ye of Too Much Faith

A common complaint of faith leaders is that their congregants "just don't have enough faith." If only they believed more deeply, then they'd be willing to take on new challenges!

36. Harari, *Sapiens*, 32.
37. Harari, *Sapiens*, 33–34.
38. Harari, *Sapiens*, 17.
39. Harari, *Sapiens*, 27.

But to deal honestly with the universe of inter-subjectivity, we must recognize that the problem is not that people don't have faith. If anything, they have too much faith. Inter-subjectivity creates a vast array of things in which we place our faith. Many people can confuse their religious faiths with other competitive faiths without realizing the difference. It is wise for a faith leader to recognize this to discern (a) how to address these competitive faiths or (b) if maybe the "competitive" faith is on the right track.

When our church was developing a capital campaign, our consultant, Frank, challenged us that we had not included a large enough mission component in the campaign numbers. "In my experience," he said, "a strong mission component actually increases giving because people see that they are not giving just for themselves."

Our concern was that the campaign was already large enough, pressing hard against our likely giving capacity. But Frank framed this as a matter of scarcity versus abundance. "If people believe that there just aren't enough resources to go around, that they can only take care of themselves," he said, "you're operating from a perspective of scarcity. But this campaign is an opportunity to get people to dream, to imagine the greater future God has in store for them and for the community."

A communal "belief" in scarcity or abundance is a matter of faith—an inter-subjective reality. The congregation had believed in scarcity for many years for good reason. But over time things had changed. Where once faithful stewardship required a level of conservatism and frugality, now the question was whether the demands of the moment, the resources available, and our hope in the future God intends required us to think from a perspective of abundance.

Frank was challenging *my* faith. Did I believe in scarcity or abundance? Clergy need to be able to see the way these competitive inter-subjective realities shape how we lead. A congregation's inter-subjective reality influences a cleric, especially after they've been there awhile.

Changing a congregation's perspective on scarcity and abundance could be viewed as simply replacing one faith with another faith. Sermons and Bible study lessons on how abundance is God's plan and giving is an expression of faith are appropriate. It is certainly possible for faith leaders to convince people to give abundantly as an act of faith, even if it is against their best interests. But we tend to look upon such leaders as charlatans.

As our goal is shared power, we must recognize that changing an inter-subjective reality—a belief held in common by a large group of people—is a major task that requires an all-hands-on-deck approach. All four frames need to be utilized in a thoughtful, strategic, and integrated fashion. Broadly speaking, an approach to a capital campaign could look like this:

1. *Symbolic Frame*: Preaching and teaching on our faith and hope in God, addressing the need in congregation and community and the vision the cleric and faith community share for the congregation's ministry in the future. Enable the congregation to see that the faith we have directs us to abundance, but make sure everything said is grounded in reality. Do not berate them for lack of faith and do not patronize them with platitudes. Our job is to convince. Use convincing, grounded arguments as well as larger faith assertions. Develop campaign materials whose strong graphics and campaign theme speak to the larger vision the campaign is addressing.

2. *Political Frame*: Intentionally build the case for abundance with key leaders in the church. In my case, for instance, I identified the people most trusted on matters of money and had one-on-one conversations with them. Many of these were also trustees, who took seriously how the church's trust was used. If trustees could be persuaded, they could use their influence to affect the opinions of the boards and committees they served and likewise educate the congregation. If the trustees were willing to invest a substantial piece of the trust into it, that would go a long way toward convincing the entire church of its benefits.

3. *Human Resources Frame*: Find out the "whys." Why are people worried about scarcity? How much does it reflect experience, both of church and life? Address their dreams: what do they hope for the church? For themselves? Make a point of addressing different groups—women's circles, the men's group, Bible studies, adult Sunday school—and take time for feedback and questions. A capital campaign is as concrete a referendum on the congregation's leadership as you can get. The pastor must prove herself trustworthy with humility and honest answers to challenging questions. This is where whatever capital she's already developed as a faith leader will make its mark. "Whoever can be trusted with very little can also be trusted with much," Jesus tells his disciples (Luke 16:10). If a congregation has reason to distrust the pastor, the initiative will have no hope no matter how trustworthy the other advocates might be.

Below I address the issue of a plan. Again, as always, your goal is shared power. No plan is shared if it is not developed via intense consultation with your congregation and its leadership. If a plan is perceived as shared, it has become a communal act of faith. You are on your way to creating a new inter-subjective reality, a story that because it is believed by many people, has power to effectuate the vision pursued. Intensive focus on both the human resources and political frames is essential.

4. *Structural Frame:* Two things, minimally, are required here, and both are critical. First, you need a plan and second, you need broad, public buy-in. The plan should be developed in consultation with the congregation, its leaders, and experts. You cannot afford to skimp on this. If it requires building renovation or new facilities, hire a church master planner. If it requires a strategic plan, hire a consultant. Each of these steps requires you to build buy-in from congregants and church leaders. A good plan in place is a major feature for a large project, easing anxiety and inspiring confidence and trust. Make sure that plan is approved and doesn't look like "your" plan but "our" plan.

   Follow all protocols. Do not skip a single step. Every shortcut is a hole in the foundation you're trying to build. Be open with the congregation at every stage and make sure your boards have approved every stage. If permission or guidance is required from higher governing bodies (not to mention local authorities) make sure you have them. When you are building or doing building improvements do not—I tell you this from experience—do not trust your own church members to substitute for hired experts "to save money"! In the first place this implies scarcity; in the second place a volunteer cannot be held accountable; and in the third place it will almost certainly go wrong and cost you three times as much as it would have otherwise. At St. Stephen, we had a building engineer serving on our property board. He was adamant that for every project we hire a project manager. He would never manage a large project himself or trust anyone else in the church to do it. He's right.

The Incredible Power of the Symbols

One cannot emphasize enough the incredible power of the symbolic. The ability to conceive of corporate myths, stories, and religion—the realm of faith—is the quality that has separated us from the animal world and our now-extinct humanoid peers. Its most striking characteristic is that it can organize large groups of people to act on an idea. It gives individuals a reason to live and a group to which to belong that transcends biological or evolutionary tribal bonds and limitations, passing on traits and behaviors to diverse groups and succeeding generations.

These benefits of the symbolic, with their evident effectiveness across ages and peoples and cultures, must force religious people to contend with our deep-set distrust in the effectiveness of our faith assertions.

In recent years, Christian thinkers have recognized some key advantages of anabaptist beliefs. Many Christians feel discouraged over the disappointing results of the Niebuhrian "Christ Transforming Culture" model that dominated late-twentieth-century theology and practice. Some theologians have asserted that effectiveness should not be the measure of true faith. The values of Christianity must be followed even if they are ineffective; indeed, they are so countercultural that they will almost certainly be ineffective in a fallen world. These theologians encourage engagement with the world, but with the caveat that we cannot assume that the values we promote will be effective. Their point is that we must abide by these values no matter what.

The concern is that often believers mistake effectiveness for fulfilling God's purpose, leading them to use immoral or amoral means to achieve what they perceive to be God's ends. That concern is justified. *But it is at least as common, if not more so, for people of faith to believe that their faith has no power in the world.* At one level this leads to otherworldly thinking. A corollary to this is the belief that the work of faithful people has no practical effect. One concern I have with the renewed interest in anabaptist principles is the implication that all the church can do is bear witness to an alternative way to live; it really cannot effect substantive change on society or culture. Taken to its extreme, this leads to acedia.

The extreme alternative is partisan Evangelicalism, which shamelessly pursues political and cultural power using the immoral or amoral tactics of the most corrupt politicians. They have unabashedly adopted the model of dominating power. Their brand of religion is extremely effective. It must be countered by an effective form of power-sharing religion to avoid the total corruption of faith in the United States.

For unifying congregations to accomplish this, we must take seriously the immense power of faith to unify, motivate, and empower God's people. We must understand that *faith is not the opposite of realism.* Everything that is considered "real"—money, property, corporations, politics—is as much a product of the inter-subjective realm as the faith of any community of believers. All inter-subjective realities have power, the ability to organize people and money. In fact, *only* inter-subjective reality can organize people and money!

It is a mistake to imagine that faith in a transcendent God who requires justice, lovingkindness, and humility is less effective and potentially world-shaking than other inter-subjective realities. The cross and the Torah carry symbolic power that far predates and has been of more consequence than any national flag or corporate logo. The question is how to harness that power to attain the goals of power-sharing and moral suasion that can have a positive effect on both our religious and secular institutions.

4

Power and Congregational Type

The Alban Institute developed models of congregation type based on form and size. We will examine each of these from the perspective of power. But I caution that congregations are changing rapidly, and clergy, congregations, and judicatories are experimenting with radically different ways to gather. This raises questions about how useful these congregational types are in describing emerging church dynamics. At some level any or all these dynamics could be at play in any congregation.

The Family-Size Congregation[1]

A young Quaker pastor accepted a call to a church of fifty-four members. The denominational office warned him that this was a church that ate pastors for breakfast. In his first meeting with the three older women who were the church's main powerbrokers, he made it clear that he was not going to cave to their pressure. As he grew the church to more than one hundred, he dealt continually with their sabotage. Throughout he courageously confronted them, asking at one point, "You know, you're going to die soon. Why are you standing in the way of the church growing and surviving after your death?" They couldn't see his perspective. To them, they weren't the

---

1. I will use Israel Galindo's designations from *The Hidden Lives of Congregations*.

77

problem, he was. After ten years, his doctor advised him for health reasons to leave ministry altogether.

The pastor's problem was that this was a family-size congregation. Family churches are closed systems. They are family. Anyone from the outside is not. This includes the pastor. Even though the cleric may have been hired to grow the congregation, it was likely impossible to do so barring a complete turnover in membership.

Family churches comprise a handful of families and their friends. They are small, often around fifty or so with worship attendance in the twenties or lower. Most church professionals think of them as "chapels," referencing the practice of well-off families in the past to build chapels at their castles or estates and hire priests or pastors to minister exclusively to them. With the decline of mainline churches, there are many such "chapels" in existence, tiny congregations with few or no resources but carrying the memory, real or imagined, of a once glorious past.

Pragmatically speaking, many of these churches should have been closed long ago, but districts and regional councils have a hard time doing it, often for sentimental reasons. These congregations have little power to affect the larger church and little power to help themselves, either.

It is true, however, that they have one thing: property. In many denominations, the regional council has ultimate responsibility for abandoned church buildings—a responsibility they would prefer not to have. There are family churches that can and do take advantage of this last vestige of power by hanging on as long as they can.

Sometimes the best role for the pastor to play in the family church is as the chaplain, taking care of the spiritual needs of the congregation. Such churches often struggle with depression and a deep sense of loss. There is plenty of pastoral work there for a chaplain to do. In the present post-COVID environment, it is realistic to anticipate that more of these congregations will emerge and ultimately die in the next ten years, leaving judicatories with the daunting problem of what to do about the property.

These congregations demonstrate the power of acedia. Emotionally they are often deep into a self-fulfilling sense of decline and helplessness. Ironically this sense of powerlessness has great power affecting the direction of the church, the attitudes of church leaders and clerics, and the responses of larger judicatories, who themselves feel helpless to change things and so leave the congregation alone, which is often what they want.

Many such declining congregations find graceful ways to exit, such as giving their building or endowment to a nonprofit. But in others the power of victimhood overwhelms their ability to act and guilts the judicatory into appeasement rather than problem-solving. Even if a congregation is dying, there are ways to enhance their ability to take control of their destiny.

The Shepherding-Size Congregation

Congregations are considered "shepherding" if their active membership is between fifty and 150.[2] This puts them in an uncomfortable place between the family- and programmed-sized, with the pastor on the hot seat. The pastor is the spider in the web in a shepherding-size church. Every vibration goes back to her. She is the center of every power struggle. That doesn't necessarily mean, however, that the pastor has any power!

The closer this type of congregation is to either of its bookends, the more pressure is on the pastor. If it is closer in size to a family congregation, then family dynamics will make her web bounce and jump. If the church is closer in size to, or aspires to become, programmed-sized, she will experience the tug of people who want to be a larger, more programmatic church, but at the same time paradoxically want to maintain the closeness and fellowship of a smaller congregation—and do all this on a shoestring. The pressure on the cleric is to balance these contradictory goals and either achieve them or take the fall if it can't be done.

These tensions pit a human resources frame against a structural frame. It requires a cleric to focus on the political frame to make any progress toward success. Many shepherding-size congregations will say they want to advance toward becoming larger and more program-oriented; but their innate comfort with being smaller, more intimate, and more family-like will inevitably pull the rug out from under attempts to welcome new members or to focus on developing structures to increase giving, maintain a budget, hire good staff, or initiate new programs (especially if it means abandoning old programs!). If the cleric focuses on developing programs or evangelizing, then many will feel like she's not paying enough attention to pastoral care of the flock she already has. If she tries to initiate new or more structured ways to do things, she runs up against powerful interests invested in "the way we've always done it" and the pastor-killing possibility of deeply

2. Galindo, *Hidden Lives*, 81.

hurt feelings. And then there's the problem of minimally invested leadership, who often believe that it's the cleric's job to do ministry, not theirs.

In some shepherding congregations, the cleric is set up to fail.

The cleric must make a choice: She must either focus on the congregation she has and make it as healthy of a shepherding-size church as it can be or she must move it toward becoming programmed-sized, which requires a bit of ruthlessness. If the latter, she must be willing to hurt feelings and step on toes and lose members and money in the short run. She also must decide how best to bring as many people along on this path as possible. This will require more than patience, pastoral care, and good preaching. She must find the constituency who is willing to take the risk and do the hard work. She may have to choose them over others who just don't want to make the trip. Often the constituency most interested in moving from shepherding- to programmed-sized are newer members, creating tension with the established core of the congregation.

Division and hurt are inevitable—and remember that your established members are the church's treasure chest. Alienating them means alienating their money. How do you make up for that significant loss? Finding a way to keep them on board could be vital, adding another challenge on the road to becoming programmed-sized.

Never mind growing the church. Even maintaining a healthy shepherding-size church requires political acuity. Changing times call for changing ministry. In my own ministry in shepherding-size churches, the generational difference between the existing membership core and potential members created uncomfortable and potentially deadly (for the church) disagreements. Childcare, for instance, was a huge issue. Parents expected much more sophisticated childcare offerings than some shepherding-size churches offered. Established members tended to consider these young parents spoiled. Likewise, younger people tend to expect change to happen at a faster rate than older folks are ready for, or a system built for long-term deliberation is ready to accommodate. Both constituencies easily become impatient with one another.

The cleric is the spider in the web in these tensions. The nature of shepherding-size congregations means clergy must be engaged or they imperil the future of their congregations. Often though, because of their discomfort with tension and mistaken notions about "not taking sides" they limit their engagement. This almost always means that the status quo wins—but ironically that means the status quo has been undermined. If a congregation alienates potential new members and new ideas, they won't maintain the status quo but undermine it. The congregation will only continue in a steady decline to death.

A pastor or rabbi seeking to maintain or grow a shepherding-size congregation needs to balance the human resources and political frames. Friedman describes the pastor's role as "define self and continue to stay in touch."[3] The leader's political role often requires differentiation, taking a strong position, rather than staying in the middle, as many prefer. But the cleric's relational role is to "stay in touch," to stay connected especially to those who feel alienated by her differentiation.

As we will see below, a distinctive mark of the next size of congregation, programmed, is its democratic nature. Developing a more democratic structure is one way to facilitate a shepherding congregation's upward mobility to programmed-size. And of course, my thesis is that promoting a democratic model of ministry is key to congregational survival in this age of decline.

But cultivating a democratic style in shepherding congregations faces some surprising obstacles. One would think that its smaller size would lend it to democratization naturally, but not so. It is still a family-like system with a patriarchal leadership style. Just as preteen children acquiesce to parents, shepherding congregations acquiesce to their chosen leaders and do not easily think of claiming equality with them. Their anxieties center on losing their familial cocoon and their declining size. These can often conflict with one another, as in the case of the Baptist pastor who was tasked with growing the church, when in reality, they needed to process their grief over the death of so many members. Family togetherness will always trump other matters in the short run.

To build a more democratic approach to ministry, patience, political and relational acuity, and clergy tenure offer the best avenues for success. Developing a democratic culture should not be hurried. Unfortunately, many clergy with that vision are unlikely to spend a long time at these churches. The clergy likely to stay longest are those who themselves appreciate and benefit from the family cocoon that shepherding congregations offer. This isn't a bad thing. It is possible both to appreciate the family dynamic of the congregation and to use that appreciation to build trust to challenge the church to head in new directions. But the risk is that the cleric becomes part of the problem, not part of the solution.

3. Friedman, *Generation to Generation*, 229.

There is great potential for pastoral abuse of power in a shepherding congregation. Often these congregations operate as self-contained units, maintaining minimal connections with their judicatories. They can be passive about leadership, preferring to leave key responsibilities to the cleric. This undermines democratization. They are more likely to be reactive than proactive. They often identify the cleric with the institution and its mission. These qualities can pave the way for an energetic authoritarian pastor or rabbi to take control. Many people will even be grateful for it—until they aren't!

It is striking that many of these congregations seem healthy over a long-term pastorate but then fall into disarray under the next cleric's leadership, who may end up with a shorter tenure. There can be a symbiotic relationship between the congregation and the cleric: he does all the work, and they cocoon him in love and security, meaning he stays awhile, and they stay stable. But when the next cleric arrives, there's no foundation of congregational leadership and an expectation that he will work as hard as his predecessor. This leads the cleric either to burnout or to high-handed leadership and ultimately congregational decline and a short pastoral tenure. Just as the congregation credits the last pastor for years of success, they will blame the next pastor when things decline. *In either case, the congregation has not learned that it is responsible for its own destiny. That is perhaps the most important marker of a healthy, mature congregation.*

The Programmed-Size Congregation

The programmed-size church can have a very large range in church attendance, from around 150 to 350 active members. As the name indicates, the programmed-size congregation develops a variety of ways to serve its congregation and community: strong children's and youth ministry; education programming; a variety of mission outreaches; partnerships with other agencies, faith communities, and institutions; and events that attract the attention of the community. To do this requires far more staff than a shepherding-size congregation has. It is common to have a full-time program staff such as a religious educator, church musician, and an associate pastor. It is also common to have full-time support staff: an administrator, a custodian, and a business manager, for instance. There might also be adjunct or part-time staff, such as a communications professional. Good staffing at both the program and support levels is essential for a programmed-size congregation to succeed.

Because of this, the cleric is more like the CEO of a nonprofit. She supervises and partners with staff to develop effective programming and set missional goals. Leadership styles may vary. One cleric might be very hands-on, requiring regular reports from staff, supervisory meetings, and staff meetings. Another might be more laissez-faire, counting on her relationships with staff to maintain collegiality, available as needed when other staff members need support. Styles differ, but there are certain key traits that the leader in a program-centered congregation must develop in relation to staff and lay leaders.

The leader must lead. She must make her goals clear and make sure her staff is aligned with those goals. These goals and this vision must be passed on to lay leaders. Of course, these goals must be shared, rather than imposed. The leader must embody them and stand firm against the natural ambivalence of the staff and the congregation in effecting these goals. A vital task of any leader is to develop goals that are shared among the body, and then remain clear and refuse to cave when inevitable resistance and ambivalence emerge. The leader's job is to stay the course, correcting for minor errors, and to make sure that the staff, lay leadership, and congregation likewise stay the course despite the inevitable headwinds and persistent second-guessing that will emerge.

The leader must trust her staff. Micromanagement is the bane of effective ministry. She must trust that her staff are experts in their fields, as she is in hers, and give them the freedom to do their jobs. Having done that, though, she needs to check in with them regularly, congratulation them on a job well done, publicly credit them for their work, help them problem-solve, intercede on their behalf in uncomfortable conflicts, talk to them privately and respectfully about problem areas, and treat them as she would want to be treated if she were in their shoes.

The leader must continue to be a pastor. A program congregation exists in the nexus between a shepherding church and a corporation church and as such the head of staff straddles two worlds. She cannot sit in the penthouse office above the fray. Pastoral care and relationship-building are still essential to her effectiveness. One distinction between shepherding- and programmed-size congregations is the pastoral role. Running a programmed-size church necessarily means you cannot be intimately involved in the pastoral concerns of all your parishioners. A lot of day-to-day pastoral care will devolve to other staff or lay leaders with empathetic gifts. But you remain the go-to person for parishioners in crisis. You especially need to take seriously your role as pastor to the lay leaders you cultivate and work with.

It is wise to create situations where you can meet with and relate to people in larger group meetings. One visit to a women's meeting is worth twenty pastoral visits. In every congregation I have ever served, I have started a weekly Bible study. That core group has kept my finger on the heartbeat of the church. Participating in other groups, teaching an occasional Sunday school class, going to a youth group meeting now and then, meeting with your visitation team, preaching on stressors in personal and family life—all these things maintain your connection to the congregation without creating the boundary issues of people expecting you to be their personal pastor when you have a whole church to run.

The leader must cultivate lay leadership. As explained earlier, leadership training is job one. This is true in any church, but it is especially true in programmed- and corporation-size congregations where lay leaders play critical roles in implementing mission and decision making.

The leader must embody the vision. If your congregation's goal is to draw in families with young children, she must be the first person to greet them at the door. If it is to have a vibrant homeless ministry, she must show up when the homeless are present, be involved in key decision-making, serve on boards of homeless advocacy agencies, and so on. And she must expect some level of buy-in to those goals from all the congregation's staff and cultivate it among the congregation's lay leaders and general membership.

The leader must embody the direction that she thinks the congregation needs to go. In 1983, one of my predecessors at my Texas church, St. Stephen, the Rev. Bill Jablonowski, "Jab," was a well-established pastor of thirty years when he saw a headline in the paper that a homeless man had died of exposure on one very cold night in Fort Worth. He contacted the pastor of nearby First Presbyterian Church reportedly declaiming, "No one will ever die of exposure in my city again!" He got their pastor, the Rev. Bob Bohl, to find financial backing to build what is now the most important provider of shelter and housing in Fort Worth, the Presbyterian Night Shelter. At that point, no congregation in Fort Worth was seriously engaged at any level in homeless ministry. Jab embodied a vision for where he thought God needed the church and community to go. Forty years later, St. Stephen is deeply involved at the congregational level in homeless outreach. Churches and synagogues throughout the community are likewise committed to this work.

A key role of the pastor of a programmed-size church—or of a church that aspires to be a programmed church—is to scout ahead to identify the future direction the congregation needs to go. This is not as easy as just saying "I think there's a need" or "the community needs this." Neither the pastor's passion nor the community's need is good enough. Jab had been at St. Stephen so long that he knew that a mission like this could speak to his congregation. If that hadn't been the case, then taking such a leadership step would have required education and training—but even then, it would need that deep awareness of what the congregation might respond positively to, and some level of trust in his leadership.

There's a complex, subtle mix of elements that goes into identifying a congregation's growing edge. But a good pastor must find it, so that the congregation isn't simply resting on its laurels, but always moving forward on its journey. History can be a strong indicator. A new cleric must consider diving into a congregation's history a major priority.

The Pressures Affecting Leadership in a Programmed-Size Church

There are certain distinctive marks of a programmed-size church. As mentioned, the program church is the bridge between the shepherding and the corporation church and as such brings some of the challenges and requirements of both. Like a shepherding church, there is more pressure on the pastor and staff for interpersonal engagement; unlike the shepherding church, that pressure can be shared with staff and even lay leadership. Like the corporation church, there is more expectation and need for programming; unlike the corporation church, your volunteer corps and your financial resources are limited. Like the corporation church, staff members have distinctive spheres; unlike the corporation church, staffers' boundaries are more diffuse. The educator and the musician may team up on programming and the pastor may teach a regular Sunday school class or do chapel for the day school. Like the corporation church, the head of staff is not the sole focus of the congregation's attention; but like the shepherding church, if someone doesn't like the pastor's preaching, she will certainly hear about it, generally from several people!

Both programmed and corporation clerics can find themselves caught in the intrigues of official and unofficial power dynamics. Such political dynamics are inevitable but have more impact on the relational side of programmed-size congregations than on corporation ones, making the balancing act between the human relations and political frames more critical.

A distinctive mark of the programmed-size church is its democratic nature.[4] It's too big to revolve around the pastor but too small to center most decision-making solely on key leaders and staff. This necessitates constant, intentional engagement of the whole congregation in key matters affecting the life of the church. The congregation is still small enough that poor communication, secrecy, or unilateral decision-making can spread misunderstanding, gossip, or distrust.

Many have pointed to the biological reality that an individual cannot know more than 150 people at a time. Since a program church is larger than 150, intentional development of cohort groups within the congregation is essential. The program nature of the church creates some cohort groups naturally, built around the shared interests of those who love music or care about mission or attend different study groups. There must be constant reflection on what cohort groups need to be created. If your congregation wants to bring in young families, it needs to create opportunities for those families to connect to one another. Without the natural "family" glue of the shepherding church, the leadership of the programmed church must constantly be attentive to creating new opportunities for the relational needs of the congregation to be met, or they will decline into a shepherding-size church without meaning to!

The democratic nature of the programmed church requires more focus on the political frame. The pastor will find herself behaving a bit more like a member of Congress, returning to the congregation regularly through individual meetings, visits with interest groups, and town halls either to develop new ideas or to cultivate interest in key projects. It is unwise bordering on self-destructive to launch any important initiative without cultivating that buy-in. Likewise, to respond to a perceived need in the congregation without first checking in for their input likely means your initiative will fail.

Corporation-Size Congregations

A thirty-eight-year-old pastor had climbed the ladder of church sizes to arrive at last at a corporation-size congregation in a resort community. Right away he "was overwhelmed by how many people wanted to talk to

4. Galindo, *Hidden Lives*, 87.

me . . . and get me on their side. They didn't want to get to know me but to co-opt me." It was an immediate immersion into how different a corporation church is from its smaller peers. The political frame defines its life, often leaving the human relations frame in the dust. With an active membership of 300 or more, sometimes into the thousands, no other size congregation deals so openly at every level with power.

Some church dynamics experts suggest that the glue of corporation congregations is the pastor's leadership. It's as if the church-size dynamic has returned to the shepherding model, where the pastor's role is central. The pastor "may be unknown by most members yet serves as an important personified symbol of this congregation's vision and character—sometimes even enjoying a kind of celebrity status."[5]

This seems especially true in patriarchal or evangelical churches, but less so in others. Corporation church members have a deep emotional investment in the senior pastor, but that doesn't mean they like her or what she stands for. For many members, their world doesn't revolve around the senior pastor. They can align with other staff and find satisfaction in other interests. The pastor becomes a distant, politically infused figure like a president or other prominent national leader. Relationships with the senior cleric are often deeply transactional, which can shock a new pastor.

The real glue of the corporation church is "the big tent," the church's ability to cater to multiple interests and constituencies. It is this diversity that drives its political nature, creating competition for resources, personnel, and corporate identity.

Identity is one of the most important matters to a corporation church. This is why the senior pastor carries so much symbolic responsibility. These churches put a premium on their reputation and their ability to make an impact on their communities. Some of the most intense political battles are over how the congregation is perceived by others, and consequently how the pastor represents the church. Such churches are expected to be "leader churches,"[6] whose voice matters in the community. But in what way will they lead? Since its public image matters so much, there is always power jockeying over what it says and how it says it. Head pastors bring their own interests and passions and consequently their own impact on the congregation's image, about which there will be intense and passionate support or frustration among parishioners, informing some of the most intense power struggles.

5. Galindo, *Hidden Lives*, 89–90.
6. Galindo, *Hidden Lives*, 90.

People join a corporation congregation for many reasons. Its identity matters because many people like the glory and security of a publicly strong, dynamic institution. Some people leave programmed- or shepherding-size congregations to join corporation ones for the anonymity the church offers. It can be a tremendous relief to know that a corporation church doesn't need you the same way that other churches do. Burnout is a choice in a corporation size church; in other congregations it sometimes feels like a necessity.

Others come for the array of services and opportunities the church offers. Families come for the day school and strong education and youth programs. Mission-oriented people appreciate a church that has vast resources and institutional clout to address community and world needs. Music lovers revel in the beauty, professionalism, and versatility that deep pockets can produce.

Local power brokers find it advantageous to be seen in corporation churches. So do those who want to be power brokers. Some of the wealthiest members of the community populate the pews.

The "big tent" nature of corporation congregations means that whatever divisions and power dynamics frame the local community play an active role in the church's life as well. One pastor found that a major division in his congregation was between families with deep roots in the community versus "newcomers," people who'd moved there in large numbers to retire and immediately wanted to play active roles in the church. "It was an old southern town that had suddenly become a bigger place," creating political turmoil that also impacted power dynamics in the church.

Power in a Corporation-Size Congregation

One corporation pastor received a visit from an "ally" who asked him to identify the "conservatives" who were to be nominated as elders so she could spread the word not to vote for them. When he refused to do it, she developed her own ballot with red X marks by "conservative" names and "better" alternates to be written in when officer nominations came to a vote. When word got out, as it always does, many people were furious.

In corporation congregations, power dynamics not only operate among officers and staff but at every level. Every political and power dynamic active in the community infuses the congregation: conservative vs. liberal, Democrat or Republican, city vs. county, economic disparities, not to mention any political issues making headlines and filling weekly town council meetings.

Furthermore, these divisions become intertwined. In one resort town, battle lines between "newer" and "established" citizens also aligned over many other axes. Newer members were "yankees" with "liberal" notions, promoting social justice, trying to "change things"; while "established" members were "traditionalists" with "conservative" values trying to maintain stability. Both "newer" and "established" members perceived the other side as power-hungry and were dug into trench warfare about the identity of the congregation.

Nothing makes it clearer that corporation churches are political animals than the role money and resources play, for good or for ill. While these congregations have far more resources at their disposal, they are still limited. This can result in bruising fights over programming, community engagement, and vision. These battles are often public and most of the active congregation will feel invested in them.

The size of the congregation makes it tempting to create a large board for the sake of representation, but one corporation church pastor warns that this makes decision-making difficult and easily leads to either the pastor or a faction having enormous power. A smaller board can be nimbler and more responsive. Focus potential leaders on the many committees, groups, and teams.

The Pastor's Power in a Corporation-Size Church

The senior pastor walks into the door of this church with a lot of implied power in the political, symbolic, and structural frames. Two things happen immediately. Either people try to co-opt her or to establish dominance over her, maybe a little of both. A mistake a well-meaning pastor can make is to misapply the human relations frame and try to be everyone's friend. Be likable, but don't imagine that likeability will tamp down their efforts. Even in smaller, more relational congregations do not make the mistake of thinking that vulnerability will make people relate to you better in a politically loaded situation. If anything, it is like blood in the water to circling sharks.

While studied neutrality can be advantageous for the first year of any ministry, that can't always be the case at corporation size churches. Their hands are in too many pots and the stakes are too high. Often an arriving pastor must deal immediately with a crisis or politically loaded situation that developed, or was left to fester, since the last pastor left. These are critical leadership tests that can frame her leadership for years to come, often requiring her to balance her own differentiation against her ignorance of the congregation's power dynamics.

In that situation, the most astute move is generally to differentiate and deal with the fallout. One pastor arrived at a largely white church at the height of the Black Lives Matter movement. The church had a unique reason to navigate challenges related to a recent police shooting. The pastor immediately took a strong public stand in support of Black Lives Matters. There was congregational and community backlash, but his bold differentiation accrued to his and the church's advantage. It made it clear that he could be neither co-opted nor dominated and furthered the church's longstanding reputation for social justice.

The temptation to use and accrue dominating power is strong in corporation-size congregations. Likewise developing shared power is extremely difficult because power struggle frames the dynamics, and the human relations frame is de-emphasized. That doesn't mean shared power doesn't exist or can't be a goal. Staff can work toward developing shared power within each of the many interest areas under the church's umbrella, where democratization of ministry can be developed among those with similar interests; at the negotiating table in planning and budgeting; in staff and leader dynamics; and in public engagement, resisting the temptation to dominate in community ministry and working as an equal partner with other congregations.

It may be that a strictly democratized style of shared power is impossible in corporation congregations. That doesn't minimize their importance or the good they do. They are for the most part good citizens making a positive impact in their communities, able to address needs that might otherwise be neglected by the community's larger political dynamics. Unlike other civic interests, they bring a uniquely moral voice to the public square, backed up by the political skill and clout to accomplish their goals. The Faith Communities Today report tells us that corporation-sized congregations have done best in the twenty years the report covered and anticipates they will continue to do so. That's good news for ministry, communities, and the kingdom of God.[7]

7. Thumma, "Twenty Years of Congregational Change," 14.

The Power of Relationships

Of the four frames, the one least emphasized in the corporation-size church is the human relations frame. That makes it the frame where, rightly applied, the most change can take place. It can be a great deal of work, but a senior pastor who focuses on relationships can strengthen her leadership and make a powerful impact on the church's ministry.

Relationship building can happen through personal meetings, certainly, but also through attending fellowship events, small social gatherings and committee meetings, regular personalized communications, even sermons targeting real issues in parishioner's lives. All these present opportunities for congregants to see their leader as a human being, and likewise for clergy to treat parishioners as human beings.

The importance of this cannot be overemphasized. In the corporation church's heavily politicized environment, trust is hard to gain but essential to building support for one's goals. Intentional focus on relationship-building can make a huge difference. Focusing on the human relations frame affects political dynamics by making them less about power and more about relationships.

One new senior pastor saw that the church's staff and finances were overstretched with four worship services happening on two campuses. Structurally it was clear that the second campus needed to be eliminated, but the worship service there was popular with its constituents and the associate pastor assigned to it was well liked. The church took pride in having two campuses.

The new pastor hadn't had time to develop the political power to make the necessary changes and so focused on relationship work. "I formed a task force and did a lot of listening," he says. The task force worked on presenting the case in a way that allowed them to "stay one church and not get into big camps." With the task force making decisions and reporting to the congregation, there was a sense that a reliable representative body was making the decisions, not the new pastor.

Recognizing the power of the associate pastor at the satellite campus, the pastor worked on his relationship with her. He shared the importance to the church of ending that location and consolidating services on one site. She told him she was intending to retire soon. They lit upon dissolving the service in conjunction with her retirement by having a closing celebration of the program and her ministry there. Both were able to concede power because through the relationship trust was established.

One family felt deeply hurt and angry by the satellite campus closure. The pastor visited them. When he left, they had become his allies. "We're not mad at you now," they told him. "We're just grieving."

"There's an irony that that personal step depersonalized the issue," the pastor says.

Throughout, the pastor was guided by insights he'd gleaned from Ron Heifetz's thesis that "what people resist is not change per se but loss."[8] "Honoring the reality that adaptive processes will be accompanied by distress means having compassion for the pain that comes with deep change."[9] He consciously built relationships with his opponents "because your opponents have the most to lose. Behind resistance to change is grief and loss. There's some value there they are trying to protect." This keen insight into human dynamics has served him well on more than one occasion.

If the political frame is about power, the human relations frame is about humility. As trust develops, people on each side become more comfortable with giving something up for the larger good. That includes the senior pastor. This is not surprising since the goal is shared power, but it is vital.

One well-differentiated pastor won a major battle in the church without seriously alienating anyone. To his surprise, a couple of elders came to him in private and asked him to do two things: stop attending meetings of the church officer nominating committee and relax his moderatorial control over board meetings. "Even though you don't mean to, you have too much influence over nominations," he was told, "and too much power to set the agenda." The pastor conceded both these points. The request to relax some structural power was an ironic recognition that his victory had solidified his political power in the church. His willingness to concede in some areas was a relational act of humility that strengthened the board's ability to trust him with this new power.

The Ivory Tower Pastor

Serving as pastor of a corporation-size congregation can be very appealing to clergy with limited people skills. It gives them an excuse to sit in an ivory tower. This will come back to bite them. They never develop the trust they need to accomplish goals or to be perceived as properly representing the

8. Heifetz et al., *Practice of Adaptive Leadership*, 22.

9. Heifetz et al., *Practice of Adaptive Leadership*, 29.

church to the community. Not only that, they also don't have their finger on the congregation's pulse and can be blindsided by people's frustrations and anger. Their best chance at a longer pastorate is if the entrenched leadership leaves them alone in their ivory tower and does ministry without them.

Some of these ivory-tower pastors can become paranoid about power dynamics. They know they're being left out but continue to operate under the illusion that their structural power is real power. This can lead to strain especially in staff relations, producing high turnover and poor morale.

The Ditch to Die In

One thing that a senior cleric in a corporation-size congregation must remember is that this institution doesn't need him! The lay leaders and large staff can operate fine without him. He is far easier to replace than, say, a good custodian. It is wise for a senior pastor or rabbi to keep that in mind. Knowing what you can lose gives you the political edge you need.

One senior pastor talks about determining what ditch she wants to die in. A well-differentiated pastor has something she's willing to put herself on the line for. But there are a whole lot of other ditches that you don't need to die in. Figuring out which is which is key to any cleric's survival.

One way to discern this is to be clear on your strategic goals, what gets you there, and what is a distraction. Everything the pastor does has political ramifications. When you have clear goals, it becomes easier to choose your fights.

Of course, there are many things that crop up that have nothing to do with your goals, but which must be dealt with anyway. Remember that you have two overarching mandates that should always guide you: your sense of calling and purpose as a person and pastor; and your need (generally) to have a long tenure and develop enough trust and political capital to attain that purpose. The balance between these two is different for each pastor, each congregation, and each issue, but finding it is essential. As you figure those things out, it will be easier to discern which ditch is worth dying in— and then maybe not die in it, but instead become a better pastor, person, and servant of the kingdom of God.

The Hybrid Pastor-Program Congregation

Even before the COVID-19 pandemic, the decline of congregations generally had led to the hybridization of shepherding- and programmed-size congregations, congregations of shepherding-size that hire staff outside of the cleric to facilitate their ministries. These camelopard congregations at their best ease the load on clergy, create a sense of teamwork, facilitate more volunteer engagement, maintain strong existing ministries, create new ones, and keep the congregation if not growing numerically, at least stable. Sometimes this dynamic develops because the church had once been larger and still has vestiges of its old structure. But it has always been true that smaller congregations will hire program staff in hopes of growing.

In an attempt to use its data to predict post-COVID trends, the FCT writes that "It turns out that most of the decline seen in 2020 came from medium-sized congregations getting smaller. This picture shows that significant attendee loss came from those congregations sized between fifty-one and 500 at a median decrease of about 12 percent."[10] If the dramatic drop in attendance since the pandemic continues, there will be more hybrid congregations, presenting new opportunities and challenges. In fact, it is reasonable to assume, based on trend lines, that hybrid-style congregations will be the norm, if they are not already, outside of corporation congregations, which have thrived the most in the twenty years of the Faith Communities Report.

Maintaining any size staff of any quality is fully dependent on finances. As attendance decreases, income decreases. Financial considerations must be weighed in staffing decisions. Since faith institutions are allergic to money, these conversations can be painful. It is wise for a congregation's leadership, lay and clergy, to do a staff assessment. Weigh hopes and dreams against resources. This may pit structural or symbolic considerations against the human relations frame. Do not make the mistake of hanging on to staff you love but can no longer afford, or whose work is no longer satisfying your missional goals.

It is common for a part-time staffer to be nonprofessional, perhaps even a congregant. Their work may not be satisfactory. It's good to manage your expectations from the get-go. What are the measurables by which you will evaluate the staffer's effectiveness?

10. Thumma, "Twenty Years of Congregational Change," 14.

There are a couple of ways to look at this. You can set goals for increased participation and/or more programs—say, twice as many teens in youth group or start a children's choir. Or perhaps you want to offset attrition or unacceptable performance. If you have no youth group, then having any at all is a win! Or you might hire someone familiar with business software because your volunteer treasurer is overwhelmed. Set reasonable and measurable goals. A youth minister who isn't a professional is unlikely to create the best youth group in the city. A part-time secretary can't be the organizational brain for two staff members and all the committee chairs.

Often the congregational serpent emerges by setting unreasonable goals for part-time staff. Personnel matters unfortunately can become opportunities for anxious power to rear its head, resulting in ambivalent and confusing messaging to staff or straight-up cruelty.

Part-time staff can be hard to supervise. Clergy and boards have less power to manage them; the staffer has more power to say no. Clergy and personnel committees may micromanage or question the staffer's work to compensate for their reduced managerial power. This undermines morale and can become a self-fulfilling prophecy. Or the staffer may feel he has you over a barrel because it's unlikely anyone else would take the job.

If you hire a congregant, you risk a political quagmire. Mutual trust may be the only foundation for the employer-employee relationship. Without it, supervision is impossible and firing, or quitting, has a deeply felt impact in the congregation.

Faith organizations often do not appreciate the political nature of hiring, supervising, and firing staff. This is doubled when hiring part-time staff. Both employer and employee have limited power. Limitations add anxiety to a system. Hybrid congregations are people-oriented and see staff relations from a human resources frame. Employers must look at staffing from the structural and political frames. How does this staffer accomplish mission and increase or decrease congregational power? This cold calculus is especially difficult in shepherding and hybrid congregations. Often the supervising cleric is gifted with people skills but uncomfortable with the politics of supervision.

Rather than strictly supervising a nonprofessional part-time employee's work, reinforce their authorship. Keep expectations loose but encourage their creativity. Brainstorm with staffers on how they think the job should be done, building on their strengths and passions. One pastor at a hybrid church discovered his part-time nonprofessional family minister was interested in starting a youth group for children with disabilities. No other church offered that option. The pastor encouraged her to learn more, find community partners and allies in the congregation, and to connect the existing youth ministry to disabled youth. He suggested a checklist of measurables and checked in with her regularly on progress, reinforcing her vision but also helping the staffer learn how to set and implement goals. This energized the staffer not only for this new ministry but for those she was already supporting. It gave the youth group a distinctive mission focus on welcoming special needs teens.

There are few areas of congregational life where the wise serpent and the gentle dove are more at odds than in part-time staff relations. Personnel committees can be demanding and part-time staff frustrating. Hybrid congregations may not always realize the challenge this creates.

On the other hand, hybrid congregations offer a creative and hopeful approach to managing adaptive change by balancing the relational qualities of smaller congregations with the program options of larger ones. One key to this is clergy comfortable with balancing management and congregational care.

Another key, however, is to focus on democratizing ministry. Part-time staff offer a unique opportunity for this. They need volunteer support. Clergy who emphasize democratization can mobilize volunteers on several fronts by training their staff in volunteer development. Sometimes part-timers (and congregational staff generally) feel morally obligated to do all the work themselves. Reframe for them that their job is not simply to get the job done, but to empower others to do the job, too. More to the point, part-time staff simply will not succeed without volunteer support.

Democratization of ministry at the very least can keep a small church vital. But additionally, it is a step toward becoming a programmed-size congregation, for whom democratization is a hallmark.

5

The Power of Individual Congregants

Some decades ago, a pastor who led in the self-assured, over-dynamized style of clergy of the day ruled the church's board with an iron hand. One elder refused to bend to the pastor's will on a key issue, infuriating him. Soon after their heated disagreement at a board meeting the elder had an emergency and needed major surgery. The pastor didn't visit him in the hospital. When he got out, he confronted the pastor. "Did you not visit me in the hospital because I disagreed with you?" he asked. "Yes," the pastor admitted, "and I'm sorry for it." While the elder respected the honesty, it did not change his opinion that the pastor's leadership was too domineering.

The elder knew that ongoing tensions between him and the pastor had potential to split the church, which he did not want, and so he chose not to return to office again. Fortunately, he was respected and loved so his voice was never fully lost, but this illustrates why self-confident, personally powerful people can feel alienated from congregational leadership.

It is hugely advantageous for clergy to cultivate good relationships with these folks. Not only do they help a pastor learn self-differentiation, but such alliances have great power to accomplish ambitious goals in the church or synagogue. Independent-minded people are more likely to think of or embrace new ideas. Of course, they are also more likely to step on toes along the way. If that quality can be stifled or appropriately directed, they can be powerful allies. With their help, the pastor can maintain her own differentiation against the inevitable pressure to conform; likewise, as strong-willed parishioners take on a more engaged role, they model for others how they, too, can be differentiated.

Clergy are often aware of and appreciate "the variety of gifts" their members and volunteers bring to the table. As a rule, though, there are even more people in the pews who really don't know their own gifts or else have no outlet for it.

Everyone has power. "Power," writes Loomer, can be "defined as the ability to make or establish a claim on life . . . Power is coextensive with life itself. To be alive, in any sense, is to make some claim, large or small. To be alive is to exercise power."[1] An essential part of human spirituality is to tap into our power and fully live.

One of the tasks of creating shared power is to help everyone identify and activate their personal power for the good of God's reign.

Spider-Man's familiar mantra is important here: With great power comes great responsibility. The fact that so many do not recognize their own power means a couple of things. For one, they don't perceive their worth in God's eyes, nor are they fully living; but for another, they likely have no conscious control over how their power expresses itself. Often their power is driven by anxiety and reactivity rather than more productive emotions. Congregational leaders must help people identify and responsibly harness their power for the good of God's reign.

There are several ways to recognize a person's power. We can look at their skills, talents, and background. But often we *experience* their real power. There are those who impress us, whom we admire and wish to be like. But there are other ways to experience someone's power. Does something about this person make you uncomfortable, challenge you, push your buttons? Do you want to avoid, minimize, react, push back? You are responding to their power. Sometimes, it is directed and controlled, like the elder who pushed back against the domineering style of his pastor (a style that also was a power). But often it is undirected, like the person whose anxiety seems so out of control you want to leave the room. In this chapter, I am asking you to reframe not only gifts, talents, and strengths as powers, but also so-called weaknesses, personality flaws, and undesirable traits as power with the potential to be used for the good of both the individual and God's reign.

One Christian educator had an extraordinary ability to identify people's power and find a place for them. In one case a family with young

---

1. Loomer, "Two Conceptions of Power," para. 3.

children were considering joining. The wife had grown up in the church, but the husband had no ties to it and had been burned in previous churches. The educator identified that what he most wanted was to be needed. She started assigning him tasks such as building a puppet stage, running the sound system for events, or bringing refreshments. He felt recognized and valued. The family joined soon afterwards.

The husband's "power" was not a specific skill set like financial or legal expertise. It was a character trait, one that might be viewed by some as a weakness: he needed to be needed.

Character traits like trustworthiness, a need to be liked, assertiveness, an inquisitive mind, and humility, rarely make it onto "Gifts and Talents" questionnaires, but often matter more than skills. A community organizer sometimes dreaded meetings with a particular volunteer because she'd likely be angry about something. "But that's exactly why we need her," he told me. "We need that anger." Anger was her superpower. More than once it served well in tough meetings with county power brokers and challenged the organization to up its game.

The need to be needed can be an incredible asset to congregations. We find it often among older members or those with disabilities who may feel useless or at loose ends. Without an outlet, it can manifest as dependency; but treated as a power rather than a liability it can reap rewards in valuable volunteer labor while also giving people a sense of purpose and meaning.

One member drove me crazy with her concern about whether the needs of the elderly members of the church were being met. She was especially concerned about communication as we turned to social media, which she viewed as alienating to older folks. After we hired a communications consultant who reported directly to me, we formed a communications committee. I asked this woman to chair it. I felt that her passion and commitment would aid our internal communications and that I could run interference for her more controlling tendencies.

She proved herself during the pandemic. During that period when we were cut off from direct contact with one another, she created a telephone tree, made up predominantly of our shut-ins, who checked in on all our church members. While only perhaps a third of the congregation responded, the ones they reached were the ones who most needed it. The brilliance of the phone tree was that many of those who most needed it were the callers! She had activated their power.

In this member's case her anxiety manifested as genuine care for a marginalized group, the elderly and homebound. It gave her a prophet's power to serve as the voice for the voiceless and put her concerns into action.

Recognizing and activating the power of all congregants requires us to pay special attention to those least empowered: children, the marginalized, the mentally ill, the poor, the elderly and disabled. They are easily missed, but often most need it.

One common mistake is to treat young adults and families as dependents and either neglect them or limit their access to power in the church. (Of course, another mistake is to imagine they have more power than they have and immediately overwhelm them with responsibility!) While it is true that younger adults, especially with children at home, are limited in time, energy, and money, engaging them is critical to the future of the congregation. Many congregations' traditional means of involvement—serving on boards or serving as a regular volunteer—are closed to younger adults. Polling them on their interests and finding "one and done" activities can give them a way in. They may not want to serve on a committee, but they might be glad to participate on a rotating security team or attend a city council meeting on an issue they care about. Personal, individualized attention can make a huge difference. Gathering their input and respecting their limitations can secure commitment and engagement.

In one case, after trying many things a staffer lighted on holding a 'theology on tap" event in the church once a month for summer and fall. To build to that point, she spent several months trying and failing at different approaches. She tried having an event at a bar, having an event weekly or monthly, making it a Bible study, asking a young adult to lead it, and so on. None of them seemed to work, but she kept trying. A key problem was childcare. Having the event on campus with childcare providers, and only at certain times a year, solved the problem. It ended up being a series of presentations with different speakers with time for discussion and the outlaw appeal of consuming alcohol in the church building. It drew both young and old, facilitating cross-generational communication, serving as a place where young adults could discuss and have influence on larger congregational concerns.

Prior to the age of Uber and Lyft, a monopoly taxi company had a stranglehold on transportation for the elderly and disabled in one community, resulting in many being late to appointments, left waiting for hours, or experiencing physical harm from neglectful or rough cabbies. Many congregations banded together to hold the company accountable. One woman in my congregation had muscular dystrophy. An impatient cabbie had slammed the trunk shut on the wheel of her walker and twisted it. When she tried to use it, she fell and broke her hip, requiring surgery and weeks of recovery. She felt helpless to respond. I asked her if she would be willing to give testimony at a public accountability event where hundreds would be in attendance. Our community organizing team trained her to write and publicly read a statement, something she was determined to do despite a speech impediment. Her testimony had a powerful effect on the crowd. It made the local metropolitan newspaper. She felt empowered and excited. This campaign resulted in an end to the taxi company's reign of terror by opening the door for several cab companies to compete and pressuring county government to make and enforce rules of behavior.

Theologian Walter Wink writes that Jesus addresses powerlessness in his disciples, who keep thinking that it is up to Jesus to change the world:

> The disciples cannot know that the messianic powers dwell in themselves as well as in Jesus. They have been taught that a powerful charismatic leader, soon to come, will possess these powers. Their job is to conform, to assent, to follow. *That these powers might be theirs as well has never dawned on them.* [Italics mine.] They have, in fact, been trained not to believe that such abilities lay within their reach. They have been taught not to seek power in themselves. The Powers want people pliant. The religious authorities tend to want their devotees passive. Leaders do not want empowered people; they want trustworthy followers. How interesting that Jesus has chosen disciples from the margins of society, people not caught up in the power game. He wants to be the torch to their tinder, to set them on fire for God: 'I came to bring fire to the earth, and how I wish it were already kindled!' (Luke 12:49). But this kindling is soggy and will require drying out.[2]

Our goal as faith leaders is to dry out and ignite the soggy kindling of our demoralized congregants who do not believe they have spiritual power within themselves to transform the world. They have been taught the "thoughts and prayers" mantra of acedia. They think they have no choice but to wait for God to change things, or else hope for the end of time. In contrast, the biblical message is "See, now is the acceptable time; see, now is the day of salvation!" (2 Cor 6:2). Christians are told that Jesus is filling us with God's Spirit so that they "will also do the works that I do and, in fact,

2. Wink, *Human Being*, 136–37.

will do greater works than these, because I am going to the Father" (John 14:12). There is nothing passive or powerless about being God's people and doing God's work. It is God's power at work in the world.

Respect Is Love

Key to understanding other people's power is respect. We relate to our congregants in many ways: like, dislike, distrust, tolerance, pity, anger, and so on. Respect has nothing to do with any of those. Respect is "to consider worthy of high regard" or "to esteem."[3] Everyone deserves respect because they are made in the image of God. Messianic power already dwells within them.

Respect means seeking the messianic power that dwells in each of our parishioners and in people in general. We can like, dislike, distrust, tolerate, or get angry at them and still respect them. We cannot respect them if we pity them. We are not respecting them if we do everything for them. The Iron Rule of community organizing is *"Never, ever do anything for anyone that they can do for themselves."* This is respect. We either let them do it themselves or teach them how to do it themselves. When we assume less of them, we are treating them with disrespect.

For all intents and purposes, respect is the most concrete expression of love. We love our neighbors by respecting them. We have confidence that they can act and make choices for themselves. As clergy we seek to enable that, whether by training them or by getting out of the way. We also want to direct it for the purpose of God's reign on earth.

We also expect to receive respect from others. Respect is reciprocal. Some people use lack of respect as a means of controlling others. They intend to create awe or fear within us. Some clergy do this; others are victimized by it. Insecure religious leaders often are susceptible to this, partially because to expect respect sounds self-aggrandizing. It isn't. You, too, are made in the image of God, infused with messianic power, and have the ability to act. To tolerate disrespect is an affront to the Image of God within you.

You have reason to think you are being disrespected when you feel put down by others. But feelings are not a good judge. We can fool ourselves. Disrespect can best be seen in actions. The church treasurer who required me to pick up my paycheck at her house was treating me with disrespect. When I missed scheduled appointments with a church member because I forgot to write them down, I was treating her with disrespect. When

3. S.v. "Respect," https://www.merriam-webster.com/dictionary/respect.

the vestry of an Episcopal church "downsized" the music budget without consulting with the music director, they were treating him with disrespect. When any faith leader teaches Bible as if they are the final arbiter, they are disrespecting their parishioners' ability to understand and interpret scripture for themselves.

Acts of disrespect are acts of power. They are often political acts and can certainly have political ramifications. Faith leaders must always be alert to the ways their actions might be disrespectful. Likewise, they must be aware of acts of disrespect directed toward them. Some disrespectful behavior isn't worth bothering with—it tells you more about that person's insecurities than anything else. You can ignore it or dismiss it or hold it as information. But some disrespectful acts require a response.

Disruptive Power and Adaptive Change

Many delegates to an annual Baptist Convention were frustrated by the dysfunction and possible corruption in their mission board. The problem was what to do about it. The mission board was independent of the convention and consequently unaccountable except through appointment of board members. The long-time, domineering chairman of the mission board had been briefly fired but found his way back to leadership again.

The night before a vote to approve the board's work was on the convention agenda, several delegates gathered and expressed frustration about how to respond. Then they received a surprise visitor—the assistant director of the mission board. He presented them with concrete evidence of mismanagement and blatant corruption. In this act of resistance, he was implicating himself as well, so it came with great risk.

His courage was an inspiration to his colleagues. The evidence he presented them was the firepower they needed to instigate change. Still, the delegates were realistic about addressing a deeply ingrown structural problem. It is always difficult to change an established structure because of the anxiety caused by the uncertainty it creates. People are more likely to demonize the disruptors than to critique the system.

Furthermore, most of the disruptors were young or little-known church leaders with no real clout or reputation, up against "the good ol' boy" system. They had no political capital. They likely would not be taken seriously, and their reputations and career opportunities could be forever damaged.

One among their number stepped up, a well-respected long-time pastor and denominational leader. The next day, he put his political capital on the line by recommending that the convention take over management of the mission board. More than a critique of the board, this upended the "hands-off" model valued by Baptists, and so represented a significant structural change. Based on the evidence the disruptors had gathered, two-thirds of the assembly voted in favor of the recommendation.

This pastor courageously used his hard-earned political and reputational clout successfully to challenge and change a dysfunctional system. It helped that he was backed up by a group that was willing to stand with him and by the great courage of the whistleblower who outed the corruption.

Disruptive power is sometimes used to impose the will of an individual or a group on the larger community. It can be used to force people to listen to a perspective that is not getting heard. In most cases, disruptors believe they are on the side of the angels. You might even agree with them. But we tend to react negatively to them because of their willingness to take their critique of our structures to the next level and demand change.

There are certain signals that disruptive power is at work. If it circumvents the conventional power structure; if other people get angry or anxious about it; if it operates by spreading rumors and misinformation; if it persistently demands answers and is unsatisfied with what it hears; or if it takes hostages, i.e., withholding money or attendance, interrupting a public activity, and so on. Bob, the trustee who would not sign a document, was holding it hostage so that his perspective could be heard.

Disruptive power emerges out of frustration. Frustration is a powerful motivator for action. Often, we find the disruptive elements in our congregations distasteful and try to quell them by creating rules to suppress them. Rules quiet the public disruption, but the frustration only goes underground. If the frustrated person is invested enough to act in a disruptive fashion, rules will not be enough to solve the problem.

Sometimes shame is used: the majority simply don't agree with the disruptive opinion. If the disruptors are only a handful of people, they might grudgingly submit to the majority opinion, or they may leave the congregation.

A disruption naturally causes leaders to be reactive. It is vital for leaders to go to the balcony to assess the nature of the disruption. An objectively helpful way to discern one's path dealing with disruption is to ask whether what's sought is *technical* or *adaptive* change. Using Heifetz's construct, a *technical change* is one for which all the tools to accomplish it are already at hand, the solutions are known, and the primary changes are to structures, systems, and procedures. An *adaptive change,* on the other hand, requires a fundamental shift in the values of an organization, learning new skills, and is more relational in nature.[4]

One church lay leader, frustrated about a minor conflagration over an attempt to serve wine at a funeral reception, came to the board with a letter on behalf of the church's women's organization demanding that the church adopt a "no alcohol" policy. The leader warned that the women's group, which was tasked with providing refreshments after funerals, would boycott that task unless this policy was adopted. Most church leaders were unhappy with this request. While it was rare, there had been church events at which alcohol had been served, such as wedding receptions and certain fellowship events.

In speaking to members of the women's organization, their main concern was that they did not wish to serve alcohol at any of *their* events. It was decided to adopt the following policy: "Alcohol may be served at church events. It may not be served to minors. Groups sponsoring events have the right to decide whether to serve alcohol at the event." This policy satisfied most parties.

In this case, the disruption was technical. All that was required was to develop a rule satisfactory to the situation. The potential boycott was avoided.

In the case of the power struggle in my former church that emerged around inviting the pro LGBTQ-rights speaker to the church, this became a matter of *adaptive* change. It demanded a fundamental shift in organizational values: should we be less welcoming to LGBTQ folks? It involved learning new things: What does the Bible say about this? What does our theology really teach us? And it was interpersonal and intrapersonal in nature: it directly affected relationships in profound ways.

In the case of adaptive change, Heifetz advises that there is no choice but to see it through to the end.[5] For instance, a simple short-term technical solution would have been to "un-invite" our guest speaker. That would have removed the pressure from the immediate situation but left it simmering to erupt in other, possibly worse ways. We chose to immerse ourselves fully into the crisis. Instead of un-inviting one speaker, we invited another.

---

4. Heifetz et al., *Practice of Adaptive Leadership,* 14–17.

5. Heifetz et al., *Practice of Adaptive Leadership,* 17.

Instead of trying to keep the tension within the governing board, we made it public and open.

When facing adaptive change, a leader's job is to let it play out to its conclusion—but that doesn't mean she doesn't act. Sometimes she has to help it along. Key to this is recognizing and respecting the power of all her parishioners. Are some people too loud but the others too quiet? She needs to make sure all voices are heard. Does one group feel threatened? The threat needs to be neutralized so all sides can be heard with respect. Are there procedural or structural problems that obstruct the crisis playing out to its conclusion? Those obstacles need to be removed. When dealing with adaptive change, nothing should stand in the way of an honest, open, and respectful debate where all issues are addressed, and nothing is swept under the rug.

And nothing is more important than for a leader during adaptive change to be a nonanxious presence.

> A nonanxious presence will modify anxiety throughout the entire congregation. The capability of members of clergy to contain their own anxiety regarding congregational matters, both those not related to them, as well as those where they become the identified focus, may be the most significant capability in their arsenal.[6]

Additionally, and critically, the leader must differentiate—make it clear where she stands. Adaptive change will rarely, if ever, leave a leader with no opinion either way. Studied neutrality is never leading. "When it comes to change," Friedman advises, "clarity may be more important than empathy."[7] You may think you're being empathetic standing in the middle, but in reality, you are maintaining the homeostasis at exactly the time when change is required.

Agitation

Community organizers put a premium on *agitation*. They mean stirring the pot—not hesitating to take a stand, express an opinion, ask hard questions, or stoke debate about what you believe needs to be addressed. Agitators drive us crazy in the church. Why? Don't we want everyone engaged in lively discussion about the present and the future? Why do we automatically

6. Friedman, *Generation to Generation*, 208.

7. Friedman, *Generation to Generation*, 3.

wish to silence them? Of course, if their agitation is specifically against a visionary or necessary course of action, that's one thing. And of course, there are those who just seem unhappy about everything. But *a major reason we wish agitators would stay in their lane is how much we ourselves are invested in the homeostasis.*

Many people who agitate are triangling the church into unresolved issues in their own lives. While this is an important pastoral point, it doesn't always mean they're wrong. And remember, too, that religious leaders themselves consider agitation a divine prerogative. We've been taught to be "prophetic" and that our preaching should "comfort the afflicted and afflict the comfortable." What's good for the preacher is good for the parishioner. Doesn't God tell Joel:

> I will pour out my spirit on all flesh;
> your sons and your daughters shall prophesy,
> your old men shall dream dreams,
> and your young men shall see visions.
> (Joel 2:28)

To frame preaching as particularly prophetic is arrogant and disavows the movement of God's Spirit among all of God's people. They, too, are prophets; and to promote shared power, clergy should encourage their prophetic voice and modulate their own prophetic self-expectations. Prophesy is a gift of the community, not simply of clergy. "To resist is a basic religious sensibility," writes theologian Kristine A. Culp. "To resist is also a call. More specifically, to resist demands naming and defying idolatry and indignity in individual, ecclesial, and sociopolitical life."[8] "The Resistance" challenges our idolatry of either our brilliant new direction or our sacred homeostasis and asks, "Is this really what God wants?"

Agitation is important for three reasons. It acknowledges democratic power; it ensures that minority voices are heard; and it keeps the organization on its toes. All the best ideas start with someone noticing what's wrong and wondering what to do to fix it. When it's the majority party in the congregation, we call it creativity, leadership, vision; but when it's the minority party we call it agitation.

Friedman tells of one pastor who reframed his critics as "the loyal opposition." The advantage of this, from his perspective, was that it made him nonreactive to their criticism and eliminated the "us versus them" polarity

---

8. Culp, "Resisting," 153–54.

that was arising in the congregation. He "conveyed that he thought their attacks on him were signs of duty rather than subversion."[9]

Strategically, though, I imagine there was another advantage. As they say in politics, "There are no permanent allies and no permanent enemies." Your opposition in one congregational conflict could be your best ally in the next.

Pastoral care is key in dealing with agitators—especially if they are agitating against you. A cynical way to frame it is "Keep your friends close, and your enemies closer." But a pastoral way to see it is that agitators are often displacing anxiety from their family systems.[10] Even lending a sympathetic ear to their personal troubles can be enough to help them overcome their tendency to personalize a disagreement with you, the church board, or another member.

It also helps if you can maintain enough distance to get in the balcony and objectively evaluate what they are agitating about. If you can see their point of view and are willing to agree openly with them on at least some things, many disagreements can be defused; but even frank discussion of why you disagree, done in a respectful way, can go far in defusing an anxious situation.

A key question in dealing with agitation is, "Do they have a following?" If your agitator has other folks on their side, you need to take the agitation seriously. If you are hearing a complaint from one person, it may be idiosyncratic. If you are hearing it from a few people, but they are talking about it separately, it's probably worth taking a bit more seriously. But if they have begun to talk to one another, or more, to get organized, even if it's just a handful, it's wise to deal with it intentionally. Get up into the balcony and objectively assess their complaint or their request. Never assume that you can dismiss it by ignoring it. Remember, the best ideas and initiatives of any organization begin with agitation.

Don't Make the Perfect the Enemy of the Good

Earlier we looked at Bolman and Deal's example of how a school system's top-down decision-making can run shipwreck on the resistance of teachers who feel they aren't consulted. This illustrates how essential a democratic approach is to leading change. From a family systems perspective,

9. Friedman, *Generation to Generation*, 210.

10. Friedman, *Generation to Generation*, 22.

resistance, which we often view as destabilizing, serves the purpose of stabilizing the homeostasis.[11] You need to give people a good reason, and a lot of opportunity for input, to do something as radical as making radical change. The more work you do to engage people beforehand, and the more respect you show "the Resistance" when it emerges, the more likely you will be able to align the system in a way to accommodate change.

Crediting agitators with the respect they are due is an affirmation of democratic power. A key reason to take agitators seriously is that our purpose is shared power. That means that we must take the opinions of others seriously. Another great political adage is "Don't make the perfect the enemy of the good." Compromise is a valid and often inevitable outcome of sharing power.

Compromise can seem especially unappealing to religious people because someone will feel that the view they represent has been handed down to them from God. To them, compromise is a dirty word. Compromise must be reframed as reconciliation, a word with powerful biblical and theological meaning. To reframe *compromise* as *reconciliation* moves it out of the political frame and into the human relations frame. Symbolically the words are different as well: *compromise* is giving something up; *reconciliation* is creating a bond between divided parties.

In one congregation, most of the board was prepared to invite homeless people into its building for food and shelter overnight a few months out of the year. In a straw vote, the pastor noted that three board members were against it. All three were lawyers and two had children that participated in the day school that met in the same building. Their concerns were about liability and the safety of children. The pastor felt their concerns were serious and should be addressed.

He had the strong advocates of the program sit down with the dissenters. One of the dissenting lawyers walked them through developing a risk-management plan for the program, pointing out that the plan not only protected volunteers, guests, and children, but also decreased liability for the church. With a risk-management plan, the dissenters were comfortable with the homeless program. It moved forward with full board approval.

Many of the program's advocates saw the advantages of the risk-management plan, but some viewed it as an unacceptable concession that treated the homeless unfairly. On the first day of the program, they tried to break some of the risk-management rules, forcing the pastor and other

11. Nichols and Schwartz, *Family Therapy*, 327.

program advocates to have to enforce them. The rebellious advocates reacted strongly to this, openly accusing him of "caving" and only "pretending" to believe in social justice. Their public disrespect of the pastor embarrassed other volunteers and served to shore up support for the compromise that had been reached. Eventually the uncompromising advocates left the church, complaining that the pastor "had won."

The problem with uncompromising ethical positions is that they see things from a dominating power perspective. If you are absolutely right, there is no middle ground; therefore, sharing power itself is unethical. There can only be winners and losers—the saved and the damned.

That is not to say that any absolute ethical perspective is wrong—only that we live in a world where there is so much more at stake in any given issue than simple black and white issues of right and wrong. It is worthwhile to note that even our most absolute ethical positions are rarely adequate if our goal is perfection. We would all agree that ideally our congregations should without compromise or prejudice welcome homeless people into full participation and parity, but that's sadly unlikely. Welcoming them one night a week is better than doing nothing at all. If we continue to make the perfect the enemy of the good, we will never make *any* progress toward our ideals. Without compromise, we will never move forward.

To reframe compromise as the pursuit of reconciliation reminds us that building community is as much an ethical imperative as any other: in fact, most, if not all, of our ethical positions are meant ultimately to build community between person and person, between peoples, and with God. This ethic of reconciliation drives our pursuit of shared power.

6

Power in Staff Dynamics

Effective Management

A SENIOR PASTOR OR rabbi is a manager. But so are staffers and in some cases even volunteers. A rabbi or pastor supervises paid employees. Often so do other staffers. All supervise volunteers, an especially challenging proposition. Bolman and Deal have key observations about what makes an effective manager. They also identify what makes an effective organization. As a rule, organizations that operate from a *paradoxical* model are most effective.

> They are loose yet tight, highly disciplined yet entrepreneurial. Peters and Waterman's "bias for action" and Collins and Porras's "try a lot, keep what works" both point to risk taking and experimenting as ways to learn and avoid bogging down in analysis paralysis. All four studies emphasize a clear core identity that helps firms stay on track and be clear about what they will not do.[1]

The emphasis on "clear core identity" is consistent with Butler Bass's emphasis on intentional practice that focuses on disciplines, values, and community.[2]

---

1. Bolman and Deal, *Reframing Organizations*, 323.
2. Butler Bass, *Practicing Community*, 83.

The above describes any effective organization from three frames—structural, human relations, and symbolic. The organization is light on its feet, courageous, and clear on its values. To create or to continue such an organization, managers need certain leadership skills. Effective managers focus on good communications and relationship building, the structural and human relations frames.[3] Internally, all staff members working on these frames will receive good marks from volunteers and employees. Most importantly, they will be doing their own jobs well!

The political frame is critical to effective management. All managers need "a significant dose of political skill and sophistication: 'building legislative support, negotiating, and identifying changing positions and interests.'"[4] Good managers at any level must deal in the political realm to be effective at their work.

When a new music director came to one church, he noted the demoralized quality of the choir. It presented him with two frameworks of challenge. At the human relations level, he needed to see to the care of his singers. At a structural level, he needed to make the choir better, but his volunteer pool had shrunk.

The solution was for the church to hire paid singers. This moved the problem into the political frame. Prior music directors had feared that the choir would become resentful of paid outsiders. It also required negotiating for more money in the music budget. He had two things going for him: the choir had become so demoralized that they were open to new approaches; and he was still in the blanket of good will that accompanies a new hire. He discussed his vision for hiring paid singers with the choir, emphasizing how they would not replace but enhance the volunteer choir and return it to the quality that it had once had—in short, all would benefit from it. Symbolically, he changed the term used from "paid singer" or "paid soloist" to "choral scholar." The choir became excited about having "scholars" (college students) in their ranks that they could mentor and befriend.

"Choral scholar" also became a selling point when he went to the board with a request for salary money for the singers. The church would be drawing college students and building a relationship with local universities. He had carefully mapped out a budget. Rather than keeping his "ask" modest—hiring two scholars, for instance—he boldly asked for four, one for each section. His boldness impressed the board. His self-differentiation

3. Bolman and Deal, *Reframing Organizations*, 13.
4. Bolman and Deal, *Reframing Organizations*, 13.

showed how fully the music director believed in his vision. His request was granted. Since then, the choir has added more choral scholars. The choir is energized and excited that they are doing the kind of music they want to do.

Throughout, the music director consulted with the senior pastor, who had the benefit of history and knowing how the system worked. The senior pastor for his part trusted the music director's judgment, gave him the autonomy to act and experiment, strategized with him on best approaches, publicly credited his leadership, and congratulated him on his vision and accomplishments.

Bolman and Deal emphasize that effective managers at every level use a multi-frame approach to address the challenges of their job. The frame you don't consider is the frame that will undermine you. Supervisors are wise to train their staff to think in frames. Using the frame model enables managers to get in the balcony above the fray to get the whole picture.

Shared Power among Staff

A supervisor must promote a sense of shared power within the staff. Not only is this because shared power is an organizational goal. It is also because staff know things the supervisor doesn't; and because mutual respect, trust, and friendship make navigating power struggles and partnering toward shared goals easier. This doesn't mean that everyone needs to be "buddy-buddy," but a supervisor is wise to promote partnering in shared projects and to make herself available in some way for key programming that other staff members oversee. Do the puppets for VBS or be liturgist for the choral Evensong. Encourage your music director and your educator to co-plan a children's worship service. When you are thinking of starting a campus outreach, invite the staff in to brainstorm. Likewise, be available to staff when they're brainstorming and encourage them to work with each other on new ideas. A supervisor must always be on the lookout for siloing, that is, programs that develop completely independent of other programming of the church. Consciously promote a balance of independence and interdependence between staff and programs.

All staff should be on the same page when it comes to shared mission goals. If addressing homelessness is a key community mission, the choir and the youth group should be on the schedule to serve dinner at the local shelter or do projects for Habitat. One church has so deeply integrated homeless ministry into its identity that its music director not only directs the highly respected church choir but also a community homeless choir as part of his job.

The congregation's staff should have its fingers on the pulse of its constituents. That includes both program and support staff. The church administrator, building superintendent, and business manager often hear things that never reach the ears of the program staff. The fact that no staff member can know everyone is mitigated by there being enough staff for everyone, and that staff communicate with one another.

Likewise, the pastor's job is to check in with staff regularly on what they hear from their constituents so they can work together to address needs or capitalize on opportunities. She must cultivate trust in the pews but also among the staff. The senior pastor may brainstorm with the educator to address an imbroglio between two teens in youth group or help the church administrator solve the problem of someone who stands gossiping at her desk for an hour when she needs to get work done. These small acts cultivate a larger sense of trust among staff so that they feel free to come to her with information that keeps her aware of the inner workings of the congregation. This is especially helpful in programmed- and corporation-sized congregations too large for her to understand without staff assistance.

The Importance of Good Staffing

Many congregations know they need staffing but struggle with the cost of it. They might spend money on good program staff but skimp on support staff; or skimp across the board on all staffing. Certain key positions may be part-time. One corollary of this is that there could be a lot of staff turnover; but just as often, once that staff is in place, they become hard to replace because the salary offered is so low. The pastor and church tolerate behavior that would get employees fired anywhere else. Complicating this are the relationships that church members form with staff, making hiring and firing a political decision as well as a structural or human relations one.

Poor staffing is a serious mistake and can have dire consequences. If the pastor feels like she can't discipline or fire employees, the poor quality of their work spills over to affect the entire mission of the church. No matter what size church you have, each employee is critical. The programs are obvious focus areas, but communication, finances, and building maintenance are mission critical as well. To underserve those vital areas is like a family that wants to focus all its energy on the joys of family life but pays no attention to the "busy work" of paying bills, home maintenance, and shopping for necessities. If those aren't addressed smoothly and effectively, all the joy goes out of being a family.

One of the most mission-critical positions is the church administrator/secretary. Administrators are the hub of the congregational wheel. Their role as communicator between staff and congregation is vital. Good administrators receive and disseminate news and information, perform essential office work keeping things orderly and up to date, form a bridge between the staff and the congregation, and are the first church representative many people meet. A good administrator is gifted with organization skills that the pastor often lacks. An administrator runs interference for staff when necessary, which means he must put off his own work to protect the staff's. A good administrator strikes a careful balance between the structural, human relations, and political frames, all the time operating with an awareness of his/her symbolic role as "the face" of the church.

A bad administrator, on the other hand, can be the death of a church's mission. He can use his relationships to church members to spread misinformation, confidential interactions, and gossip. He can shore up power and build alliances against staff or policies he doesn't like. And he can just be bad at his job, making the staff look bad and undermining the program of the church. He can use the political clout he's cultivated to hold a meek pastor and staff hostage so he can't be disciplined or fired. Good staff could become frustrated and leave, but the bad administrator stays on.

Other staff can do many of these same things, of course, and many do. But few can have the impact of the church administrator, which illustrates exactly how important this position is.

Heads of staff need to recognize that problem staff at any level is their problem to solve. That's what they're hired for. Church politics can make it difficult for pastors to see this. Often personnel committees or boards do not entirely trust their pastors or rabbis with supervisory responsibilities and second guess their decisions. Also complicating matters is the fact that few clerics are comfortable in conflictual situations.

Staff supervision is a learned skill. There are some essentials that can help with this. A good personnel policy is a great help, likewise good job descriptions. They can provide a road map and protect an employer from fallout. But as I've mentioned, the structural frame is no solution. Furthermore, not every employer has a good personnel policy or job descriptions (a problem that needs to be immediately remedied!).

For faith leaders the shift required is out of the human relations frame and into the structural and political frames. They need to learn to be objective rather than subjective. Structurally, all staff behavior is subject to the larger mission of the congregation. When one is considering disciplining an employee, a common response from congregants is that faithful people should be compassionate and forgiving. No doubt many supervisors themselves feel the same way. The question supervisors should ask is: *How is this staff person's behavior influencing the mission of this faith community? Is it furthering God's work or tearing it down?* Step away from the feelings of shame or fear that often come with making such difficult decisions and consider the bigger picture. There is an objective reality that the good of the whole outweighs the good of the one.

Often remedial steps are all that is necessary to get an otherwise good staffer back on track. But a supervisor must objectively weigh the full impact of a staffer's behavior on the larger mission and be realistic about how the mission is furthered or undermined. A key indicator is how the staffer's behavior is influencing other staff and volunteers. Is morale undercut? Have they, by their behavior, made themselves the issue rather than the mission? These are just a few indicators that the structural integrity of the mission is threatened.

Shoring up the political frame is essential, especially in a shepherding- or programmed-style congregation because relationships are so critical. *It is also vital because one of the most salient indicators of a staffer's bad influence is how well they have developed their own power base.* In many cases they have built up relationships with various key individuals or groups—the chair of the board, monied members, the women's group or particular people critical of the way the church is run. Sometimes they've created a sense of dependency that makes it hard for some to imagine how things will work without them. They may have spread rumors that make the supervisor or staff look bad, undermining pastoral authority and raising the question of whom to believe.

Often the person has a dominating personality, making many power-averse congregants easily swayed by his insistent arguments. Bullying and highly emotional behavior are unfortunately very effective in congregations. They can also be effective in cowing a supervisor. Supervisors must be especially alert to how a staffer may be bullying them, or attempting to overwhelm them with emotional behavior, because these are clear signs that this person is toxic. Objectively, it is more evidence for your case.

The supervisor should present her objective analysis of the staffer's behavior to key people to shore up her case—the personnel committee and/or the board as appropriate. Assuming that dynamics in the congregation are overall healthy, little more need be done. Normally, a member of the personnel committee should be present as witness to support the supervisor in either a disciplinary situation or a firing.

In cases of harassment, bullying, or sexual impropriety it is especially important to walk the fine line between respecting confidentiality of victims but making public the nature of the offense. Law enforcement may need to be informed.

Congregations (and pastors) do not like conflict and handle it badly. They tend to downplay bad behavior and focus on the positive, often obscuring reality in the process. This is how congregations fool themselves into thinking they can avoid "politics." A manipulative person can play off these weaknesses easily.

Empire Building

It is not uncommon for staffers, especially long-time employees, to build little empires in their congregations. The employee may be a good person, good at her job, well-liked, and overall, a benefit to the mission. But power held by anyone to this degree can be problematic to the leadership of the church as they look at the overall picture of its mission. It is not uncommon for the music program, for instance, to receive a larger share of the budget than any other program and for the music minister to have a strong personality and be a vocal advocate for the cause.

Contrary to the way some would view this, I do not see staff or members who have power as a problem in themselves. As a rule, this power means they're good at what they do. It is a net gain for the congregation. The problem comes when it conflicts with other aspects of mission. The uncomfortable reality for the senior pastor as staff manager is that she must sometimes challenge an otherwise effective staffer on how they are accumulating or using their power. The manager's job is always to promote shared power directed toward the larger goals of the congregation and to redirect misdirected power and people. No one likes it, sometimes it doesn't go well, and it rarely feels good, but that's the job.

Power struggles inevitably emerge in conversations about shared power. In this, churches are no different than any other organization. When people complain about politics in church, this is often what they mean. Power struggles are not fun, but they are a normal part of any community's life. Successful outcomes depend on mutual respect.

Whenever there is a power struggle between staff or ministries of the congregation, establishing mutual respect is the baseline. Often those aligned on either side believe their interests (and maybe themselves personally) are not being shown the proper respect. Likewise, when one side simply overwhelms another side in a situation where shared power is the goal, the damage to the loser's sense of respect can be devastating to the congregation, causing rifts and divisions.

7

Principles of Power in a Congregation

At this point it is worthwhile to point to the broad goals of the use of power in a community of believers.

1. *The purpose of shared power is to effect the reign of God on earth.* Please note the use of the word "effect." Not *affect*, to somehow *influence* the reign; but rather *effect*, to make it a reality—as Jesus taught in the Lord's Prayer, "Thy Kingdom come, thy will be done on earth as it is in heaven." This may sound grandiose. But it is my belief that our dismissal of power has made God's reign ineffective on earth, and in the process undermined our purpose as believing communities.

   The Talmud says that "It is incumbent upon us neither to bring about the Kingdom nor to desist from pursuing it." We will never fully achieve God's goals of justice, peace, harmony and *shalom*—total well-being—on earth until the time when God brings it about in full. But we believe that God has called communities bearing the Divine Name ceaselessly to pursue these larger goals, both as a witness to God's intentions for humanity and, as Jesus framed it, sowing the yeast of God's reign that will in time yield a feast for the world.

   We can change the world. This is because God has given us authorship (see 5h) and, as Wink tells us, we have the messianic power within us. God's work can be done on earth, whether by creating small communities of peace and harmony within our congregations or by working with other like-minded groups to bring about changes in our communities, nation and world. These will *not* ultimately be God's kingdom. But by working together as communities bearing the Divine Name, we can do more than we can ask or imagine—and it's time we did, in the process bearing witness to the world of God's love and justice.

2. *Our goal is the Beloved Community.* We dream of tearing down the barriers that divide humankind from one another, nature and God. Our dream is of a community of equality, shared prosperity, spiritual enlightenment, and peace—God's *shalom*. That means that:

3. *Our goal is shared power.* Shared power means first, that the entire congregation feels invested and participates in the corporate goals of the faith community. They are not doing this "because the rabbi wants to" or because "the bishop made us." They are doing it because they want to do it. They believe in the goals of the congregation and feel that they are a part of those goals.

   Secondly, we share power with other faith communities, agencies, corporations, branches of government, nonprofits, etc., in working toward goals we agree are best for our community as a whole. Shared power is not dominating power: that is to say, our goal is not to defeat an opponent, though that may be necessary, or impose our will on others purely for self-aggrandizement. Our goal is to build consensus and to empower the disempowered so that we can work together toward goals of mutual interest, for the good of the larger community, consistent with the goals of our faith.

4. *Everyone has power that must be respected.* For power to be shared, we need to recognize that everyone in the congregation has power to share. Our assumption that all power is bad has blinded us to this fact. We need to recognize the power each individual and group has.

   Furthermore, we should respect each person and group for the power they have. This is part of the lesson Paul gives in 1 Cor 12 where he says, "Now you are the body of Christ and individually members of it" (12:27) and that "To each is given the manifestation of the Spirit for the common good" (12:7). Power takes as many forms as there are people and alliances, formal and informal, in your congregation. It is wise to recognize that power and respect it, so that it may be utilized toward a shared purpose. To disrespect a person or group's power has consequences.

5. *Power should be shared, not hoarded.* I do not mean by this that an absolute democratic or congregational model of governance is best, or even good. But I do mean that whatever decisions are made should as much as possible represent the properly discerned moral will of most of the people. There are many nuances to this. In my tradition our council is directed to seek the "will of Christ" even if it puts them at odds with the majority. That is appropriate. But that same body is directed to "discern" the will of Christ. Its job is to know as well as possible what is best for the congregation, which certainly includes having one's finger on its pulse.

There are several corollaries to the assumption that power should be vested in the whole body of believers:

A. *Power is NOT solely vested in a group, groups, or individual, including the pastoral leader.* Even in a representative-style government, it is unwise to invest, or imagine you have invested, power in a council or board. Power is spread throughout a congregation. Even if a board or individual has official power, there are plenty of strains of unofficial power.

B. *Theologically, both for Christians and Jews, there is strong precedent for understanding that God is present in the midst of the congregation.* The entire arc of the Bible could be viewed as an answer to the question the children of Israel asked in the desert: "Is the Lord among us or not?" (Exod 17:7). From a faith perspective and a practical standpoint, the answer is yes, in the community of believers. Well thought-out corporate decisions are more representative of the will of God than decisions of individual leaders or boards.

C. *It is immoral for power to be solely vested in councils, groups, or individuals.* The goal is shared power, and hoarded power needs to be rooted out or regulated. Still, there are times when a properly appointed board or leader must make executive decisions that are out-of-sync with the expressed will of the majority, which leads to the next corollary:

D. *Power is shared through education.* Training and education must be constants truly to share power. If one sees a difficult decision coming up, educating the congregation about it is essential. It's better to educate before a decision than afterwards.

But if a hard decision must be made on short notice, then the congregation must be informed and educated about it openly as soon as possible.

E. *Power is shared through training.* Not everyone in a congregation wants to lead, but everyone needs to have the opportunity to learn how to lead.

F. *Power is shared through listening.* It is a mistake to believe that educating or training means telling people what to do. It also means listening to what they say. If a board is informing the congregation of a decision it needs to make, it is wise to listen to the response before implementing it.

G. *Dissent is also a power, and it has a right to be exercised.* The repression of dissent only leads to it going underground where it has powerful unconscious potential. Repressed disagreement has the same power in a congregation as Freud's concept of the id, the unconscious, has over the individual. There must be outlets for dissent to be expressed. In a best-case scenario, dissenters feel respected and continue to feel part of the congregation. In a worst-case scenario, they will leave. Leaving is also a power and must be respected.

H. *Power is shared through authorship.* Authorship, an individual's sense that they have the power to act on their ideas, is essential to instill in congregants to foster leadership and investment in the work of the whole.

6. *Shared power is corrupted by secrecy.* This is one of the most important distinctions between shared power and dominating power. Dominating power starts from the concept of war. There is an enemy to be confronted and overcome. Secrecy becomes a critical strategy so that the enemy can be surprised and unprepared to respond. Secrecy to your constituency ensures you aren't defeated from within.

Shared power's goal, however, is to build community. There are no enemies. There may be short-term strategic reasons to keep something under wraps until the time is right; but long-term or deeply held secrets are corrupting, self-serving, and destructive.

7. *There is no such thing as leadership without power.* This may seem contradictory in faith communities where servant leadership is promoted.

In communities outside the church or synagogue, of course, this statement goes without saying: Leadership is the exercise of power. In the church, however, power is looked upon with suspicion. In many cases people join a church because of a sense of powerlessness.

But as Bolman and Deal observe, "Leading is giving. Leadership is an ethic, a gift of oneself."[1] Framing it this way is helpful for faith communities. But one needs recognize, first, that one has something to offer. A leader recognizes her power and chooses to use it for the good of the larger community. There is no contradiction between servant leadership and the conscious and intentional use of moral power. But there is also no contradiction between leadership and the immoral use of power. Leadership requires power, period. The distinction is *how* the power is used.

8. *There will be winners and losers.* I once asked a group "Whom would Jesus exclude?" Many responded, "Jesus wouldn't exclude anybody! He welcomes everyone!" But that isn't true. Jesus's teachings and expectations of followers necessarily excluded people. He was critical of hypocritical religious leaders, impatient with compromisers, and threatened hellfire to those "goats" who did not realize that "whatever you do for the least of these you do to me." Despite his teaching that "When I am lifted up from the earth I will draw all people unto me," many people were *not* drawn to him and rejected him outright.

In pursuing shared power, we all wish we could bring everyone along. But we simply can't. To pursue certain goals, welcome certain people, and embrace certain values will necessarily *exclude* certain other people, goals, and values. People will feel angry, left out, and hurt. People will resist. It will get unpleasant, even dirty. You will be shocked, hurt, and angry yourself. You might lose because the only fight worth having is a fight worth losing. People will leave. You will feel terrible. It comes with the territory.

---

1. Bolman and Deal, *Reframing Organizations*, 415–16.

8

What Makes a Good Leader?

CREATING SHARED POWER REQUIRES creating strong leaders. Whether leaders are in the pews or in the pulpit, here are the essential things they need to know. Many of the technical skills, such as working in teams, fundraising, or developing and implementing SMART goals, are better addressed in other places, but they are vital. I am aware that training officers in all these skills is almost impossible. Nonetheless, these are the things they need to know. The overall goal of congregational leadership in this moment is *developing and implementing shared power in congregation and community in a time of adaptive change.* To do that, these are the qualities required.

1. *Leaders need to differentiate but stay in touch.* Leaders must understand the difference between fused behavior and a servant attitude. They must understand themselves well enough to recognize how their own family and personal dynamics may play out in an unhealthy manner in their congregations. They need to be comfortable enough with their power to express and advocate their frank perspectives but servant enough to accept it when things don't go their way.

2. *Leaders must be servants.* Servant leadership is *service to God and neighbor through enhancing the power of the congregation or institution one serves.* Facilitating the faithful will of congregants is part of the job. Visionary ideas and tough questioning of assumptions are part of

the job, but the goal is always to make the congregation effective at its mission. Ergo:

3. *Leaders must know the mission, values, and history of the congregation.* They must be able to link their work to these critical qualities, which are the symbolic sources of shared power. Leaders must also be able to assess when any of these need to change.

4. *Leaders need authorship.* They must recognize their power to lead and create and inspire that in others. Clergy, congregants, and other leaders must affirm their authorship.

5. *Leaders must be able to work in teams.* Shared-power leaders need to be able to work and play well with others, submit themselves to the larger mission, and find pleasure in that cooperative process.

6. *Leaders have followers.* Leaders need to be able to *organize people.* No one is a leader if she is standing way out in a field by herself. Nor is someone a leader who goes whichever way the wind blows. A leader persuades others to follow her. A leader must be trustworthy rather than manipulative. *You have no power if you cannot share it.*

7. *Leaders must understand the business of the institution.* Leaders must know the polity and structure. But more: they must be able to *organize money and resources.* This includes honest assessment of resources available to devote to mission, realistic analysis of staff and facilities, and fundraising. It's also wise to provide them with a list of recent decisions and actions, as well as anticipated issues for the coming year.

8. *Leaders must be able to "go to the balcony."* They must objectively assess what's going on around them, shedding their own feelings and those of others, to be able to look at the big picture. This requires that:

9. *Leaders must be non-reactive.* No leader should submit to kneejerk reactions—your own or those of others. Leaders must be able to recognize what triggers reactivity in them and the congregation and be able to hit the pause button.

10. *Leaders must be adaptable and lead adaptation.* This includes realistic assessment of what works and what doesn't work, what is possible and needed—the ability to go to the balcony—and the ability to weather criticism and stay the course for the sake of the larger mission. The ability to adapt includes the ability to reframe, a basic awareness of congregational dynamics, and the ability to assess the real needs and

possibilities of congregation and community—once again, the ability to go to the balcony.

11. *Leaders must be able to implement ideas and assess their progress.* They need to be able to organize people and resources to accomplish missional goals and to be SMART about it: specific, measurable, achievable, relevant, and time-bound.[1]

---

1. See, e.g., "SMART Goals."

Bibliography

Barnett, Victoria, and Barbara Wojhoski, eds. *Letters and Papers from Prison*. Dietrich Bonhoeffer Works 8. Minneapolis: Fortress, 2010.

Bolman, Lee G., and Terrence E. Deal. *Reframing Organizations: Artistry, Choice, and Leadership*. Hoboken, NJ: John Wiley & Sons, 2021.

Bridges, Flora Wilson. *Resurrection Song: African-American Spirituality*. The Bishop Henry McNeal Turner/Sojourner Truth Series in Black Religion 16. Maryknoll, NY: Orbis, 2001.

Butler Bass, Diana. *The Practicing Community: Imagining a New Old Church*. Herndon, VA: Alban Institute, 2004.

Burge, Ryan. "Why Evangelical Is Becoming Another Word for Republican." *The New York Times*, October 26, 2021. https://www.nytimes.com/2021/10/26/opinion/evangelical-republican.html.

Culp, Kristine A. "Always Reforming, Always Resisting," In *Feminist and Womanist Essays in Reformed Dogmatics*, edited by Amy Plantinga Pauw and Serene Jones, 152–68. Louisville: Westminster John Knox, 2006.

Frankl, Viktor E. *Man's Search for Meaning*. Boston: Beacon, 2006.

Friedman, Edwin H. *A Failure of Nerve: Leadership in the Age of the Quick Fix*. New York: Church, 2017.

———. *Generation to Generation: Family Process in Church and Synagogue*. New York: Guilford, 1985.

Galindo, Israel. *The Hidden Lives of Congregations: Discerning Church Dynamics*. Herndon, VA: The Alban Institute, 2004.

Goldberg, Michelle. "The Empty Gestures of Disillusioned Evangelicals." *The New York Times*, December 6, 2022. https://www.nytimes.com/2022/12/05/opinion/trump-evangelical-leaders.html.

Harari, Yuval Noah. *Sapiens: A Brief History of Humankind*. New York: Harper, 2015.

Hauerwas, Stanley. *A Community of Character: Toward a Constructive Christian Social Ethic*. Notre Dame: University of Notre Dame Press, 1981.

Heifetz, Ronald, et al. *The Practice of Adaptive Leadership: Tools and Tactics for Changing Your Organization and the World*. Boston: Harvard Business, 2009.

King, Martin Luther, Jr. "Remaining Awake through a Great Revolution (31 March 1986)." In *A Testament of Hope: The Essential Writings and Speeches of Martin Luther King, Jr.*, edited by James Melvin Washington, 268–78. San Francisco: HarperSanFrancisco, 1991.

Bibliography

Kinnaman, David, and Gabe Lyons. *Unchristian: What a New Generation Really Thinks about Christianity . . . and Why It Matters.* Grand Rapids: Baker, 2007.

Kristof, Nicholas. "America Is Losing Religious Faith." *The New York Times,* August 23, 2023. https://www.nytimes.com/2023/08/23/opinion/christianity-america-religion-secular.html.

Loomer, Bernard. "Two Conceptions of Power." *Process Studies* 6 (1976) 5–32. https://www.religion-online.org/article/two-conceptions-of-power/.

Nichols, Michael P., and Richard C. Schwartz. *Family Therapy: Concepts and Methods.* Boston: Allyn & Bacon, 1991.

Norris, Kathleen. *Acedia & Me: Marriage, Monks, and a Writer's Life.* New York: Riverhead, 2008.

Presbyterian Church (USA). "2012 Summaries of Statistics—Comparative Summaries." https://www.pcusa.org/resource/2012-summaries-statistics-comparative-summaries/.

———. "2021 Comparative Summaries." https://pcusa.org/site_media/media/uploads/oga/pdf/2021_stats_comparativesummary_update06_2022.pdf.

Ricks, Thomas. *Waging a Good War: A Military History of the Civil Rights Movement, 1954–1968.* New York: Farrar, Straus & Giroux, 2022.

"SMART Goals." https://www.mindtools.com/a4wo118/smart-goals.

Smith, Gregory A. "More White Americans Adopted than Shed Evangelical Label during Trump Presidency, Especially His Supporters." https://www.pewresearch.org/fact-tank/2021/09/15/more-white-americans-adopted-than-shed-evangelical-label-during-trump-presidency-especially-his-supporters/.

Thumma, Scott. "Twenty Years of Congregational Change: The 2020 Faith Communities Today Overview." https://faithcommunitiestoday.org/wp-content/uploads/2021/10/Faith-Communities-Today-2020-Summary-Report.pdf.

Wimberly, John W. *Mobilizing Congregations: How Teams Can Motivate Members and Get Things Done.* Herndon, VA: Alban Institute, 2015.

Wink, Walter. *The Human Being: Jesus and the Enigma of the Son of Man.* Minneapolis: Fortress, 2002.